ROGER,

I'm PULLING

FOR YOU—

—Kerry '96

# MASTERING THE GAME:
## The Human Edge in Sales and Marketing

Kerry L. Johnson

Published by the Louis & Ford Co.

Library of Congress cataloging in publication data
Johnson, Kerry L.
*Mastering The Game:*
The Human Edge in Sales and Marketing
87-081240
ISBN 0-9618535-0-6

Printed in the United States of America

To my father, Bill Johnson, who has contributed to my career for years, and to my mother, Jo Ann, who never stops sharing her encouragement.

# TABLE OF CONTENTS

**Game Strategy 1: How to Gain the Psychological Edge**

1. Dealing With the Fear of Success   11
2. Motivating Yourself – Permanently   25
3. Overcoming Call Reluctance   33
4. Type A/Type B Behavior: Are You Burning Out?   47
5. How to Stamp Out Stress   53

**Game Strategy 2: How to Get Inside Your Customer's Mind**

6. Subliminal Selling Skills   67
7. Psychologically Sliding Your Prospect   85
8. Gaining Your Client's Trust   91
9. Discovering Your Prospect's Buying Strategy   101
10. Influencing Sales with Color   111
11. Using Image to Increase Production   119
12. Hidden Persuaders   125

**Game Strategy 3: How to Get People to Buy**

13. Buying Signals   135
14. How Women Can Win in Sales   143
15. How to Get Trust on the Telephone   151
16. "Listen" Your Prospect into Buying   161
17. Persuading People to Buy   175
18. How to Use Referrals   189
19. Overcoming Any Objection   199
20. Closing Techniques of the Big Hitters   211

**Game Strategy 4: How to Develop People Who Will Produce**

21. Building Your Management Skills   235
22. Interviewing for the Truth   243
23. Praise: Developing Superstars   249
24. Five Steps to Great Presentations   255
25. Five Characteristics of Peak Performers   261
26. Advice to the Saleslorn   271

# PREFACE

In 1977–78, I received the great opportunity of playing professional tennis on the worldwide Grand Prix tennis tour. My claim to fame is that I was defeated by the best. Although I was relatively highly ranked, I left tennis to continue my education in business psychology. At one seminar a few years ago, an attendee stood up in the middle of the group and asked, "Kerry, why did you leave pro tennis?" I thought about an answer for a moment or two and replied, "Because I wanted to go back to graduate school." He then confronted me by saying, "No, you left because you weren't good enough, right?" I guess he was correct. If I had been number one or two in the world tennis rankings, I probably would have kept playing (look at Jimmy Connors). But yet, tennis was likely the best training ground available to prepare me as a business speaker.

On the tennis tour, we all were able to serve a tennis ball through a concrete wall. We all had a backhand that could burn marks on the asphalt playing surface. Everyone of us also knew that on any given day, whoever wanted the match badly enough and had the "psychological edge" would win. I saw many examples of world class players with the best strokes and quickest feet lose to those who were more "mentally tough." *"Mastering the Game: The Human Edge in Sales and Marketing"* is an appropriate name for this book. The game of business is not composed solely of selling the best product (although it must be at least good) or possessing technical knowledge of how it works. The game is mastered by learning how to deal with people. If this were not true, all products would be sold by direct response mail with no human interaction. I once asked a president of a major financial services company if he had the best product. He said, "No, and I don't want it. Companies with the best products go bankrupt. If we made the best widget, we would incur costs that would increase our overhead so much, we would lose money. But we do have the best people. That is why we make money." Most companies now spend 90 percent of training time educating their sales and marketing people in *technical product knowledge* and only 10 percent of the time, if any, in *technical people knowledge*. But yet, 90 percent of the same sales and marketing professionals' time is spent using their *people knowledge* and only 10 percent utilizing their *product knowledge*. You are probably a victim of your company's training practices. When your people skill level is at least equal to your technical skill level, you'll be more productive and profitable.

I recently spoke to about 400 salespeople at a conference called the International Forum. Most of these pro's had a $500,000 or more net income level. After the meeting, I talked informally to the most successful of the crop. With commissions of over 5 million dollars annually, all of them agreed that the real reason behind their wealth and achievement is their personal ability to develop strong, trusting relationships. The book is focused on helping you develop business and personal relationships. It will help you gain trust and get through to people on their level. For the past few years, my articles on people skills have appeared regularly in magazines like, *Broker World, California Planner, Midwest Planner, Life Association News, Franchise, Executive Life, Real Estate Today, Manager's Magazines, Financial Service Times, Financial Planning, Business to Business, Research* and *Communications Consultant*. Most of the hundreds of letters I receive applaud the concise, succinct, and direct ideas that are presented on dealing with people in business. The only criticism I receive is when the columns are too long or continue a concept over 2 or more months. With this in mind I organized *Mastering the Game* in self-contained chapters. Rather than reading four or five chapters to get to the point, this book presents transferable business ideas on each page. Because of this, it should be read a chapter a day over one month. Take this book to training meetings, share the ideas. If you teach each concept to just three other people you know, you'll retain these skills for the rest of your life.

Most of the concepts you read are based on university and professional level research. There is very little arm-chair philosophy. Because of this, you will gain new concepts, not warmed over sales and marketing ideas from twenty years ago. Most of the points you will read about have been tested by top producers as to their validity and applicability. You will be exposed to four game strategies in dealing with people: *1) How to Gain the Psychological Advantage 2) How to Get Inside Your Customer's Mind 3) How to Get People to Buy 4) How to Develop People Who Will Produce*. Each strategy is geared to help you with each phase of sales and marketing.

This book is the result of over seven years of research verified by thousands of seminar attendees. Primarily, I am a speaker. I speak between one to three hours at over 150 engagements each year. I present concepts that participants can use immediately to increase production. These ideas are constantly spiced with one-liners and stories punctuated with audience participation. Johnny Carson once said, "People will pay much more to be entertained than they ever will to be educated." I've never lost sight of this philosophy. While you won't be able to participate with the audience, I do hope you gain valuable ideas that will help you achieve your goals and be entertained a little in the process.

Kerry L. Johnson
P.O. Box 3665
Tustin, CA 92681-3665
(714) 730-3560

## GAME STRATEGY

# I

---

# HOW TO GAIN
# THE PSYCHOLOGICAL
# EDGE

# PART I

## DEALING WITH THE FEAR OF SUCCESS

Have you known people who looked as if they'd make tomorrow's headlines, individuals who showed great potential but who never realized their great expectations? These fallen stars may have been suffering from fear of success. Who, you may ask yourself, would ever fear success? Yet this fear is one of the most disastrous of all the fears we experience in our lifetime.

The fear of success prevents us from achieving or accomplishing our maximum potential. It limits our foresight and keeps us from attaining our production possibilities. Indeed, people suffering from fear of success believe they shouldn't be doing as well as they do now. They think they're gaining too much success too rapidly. They would actually feel better if their success rate slowed down a bit. A warning for these fearful individuals comes from an often-quoted statement, "Beware of what you think you want, because you just may get it!""

## NEGATIVE THINKING

Fear of success sufferers tend to think in such adages as:
"It's more difficult to stay on a fast horse than on a slow one."
"Beware of getting too much too fast."
"There's no such thing as a free lunch."
...and, of course, their favorite one,
"This good fortune just can't last."
Achieving a high level of success in a short time makes fear of success sufferers just plain uncomfortable.

While many individuals, including some psychologists, think of fear of success as basically a confidence or self-esteem problem, it's more deeply rooted than that. Fear of success results from having a preconceived notion of just how difficult things are, or how tough it is to attain desired goals. When we don't meet with the problems we anticipated along the way, we may sabotage our own production.

At first we feel happy with these outcomes, and have a great sense of accomplishment. But gradually, if we're suffering from the fear of success, we become anxious, and sometimes even quite upset. Psychologically, we are unprepared to deal with this sudden onset of success. We literally have too much success too fast.

What are the classic signs of this fear of success? While symptoms may vary, the experience generally is similar to those of a local real estate agent. He told me that he had generated a great deal of business by using direct mail. After continuing this successful method for more than a year, he abruptly stopped using direct mail. As we talked further, I asked him what it was that didn't work for him with this method. He replied, "It *did* work. In fact, the effort created at least a 35 percent increase in my business that year." My next question, "Why did you stop?" brought a shrug of his shoulders and a quizzical frown. The simple truth is that the direct mail tactic worked only too well for this real estate agent. In fact, it worked so well it made him uncomfortable. It brought him success beyond his wildest dreams.

You may be a victim of fear of success if you find yourself suffering from any of the following symptoms:
- Your business is not growing nearly as fast as it did when you first started in your job.
- You are failing to follow up on the leads or referrals you receive.
- You find that once you achieve a long-awaited goal, it's not as satisfying as you thought it would be.
- Even though you know that, for the best results, you should follow up on a direct mailing, you fail to do so.
- You feel as if you've reached a plateau or complacency level.
- Your income is greater than that of your parents.


## WHERE DO YOU STAND?

Now, ask yourself these questions:
- When you finally get something you want, do you find you don't want it as much?
- When you reach a goal that you have been striving for, do you think, "Is that all there is?"
- Can you accomplish something only if there is a deadline?
- Can you accept praise openly and directly, or do you downgrade compliments?
- Do you have the overall feeling that things could be better for you?

If you said "yes" to any of the preceding questions, you may be experiencing "the fear of success." By success, I don't mean high income, fame, power, prestige, or possessions, although these could be the trappings. What I am talking about is internal success—getting to do what you really want to do in your business and personal life, doing it well, and feeling good about it. The fear of success, then, is an inability to get what you want because you unconsciously feel you don't deserve it. Before you say, "Oh no, I deserve all that is good in life," read on.

## SELF SABOTAGE

Last year I worked with a bright, motivated saleswoman who appeared to be sabotaging her income because of an unconscious fear of success. This woman, a former schoolteacher, was new to the brokerage industry. As a schoolteacher, she made $24,000 a year. In her first six months as a broker, she made $21,000. Guess how much she made the last six months of the year? You guessed it—$3,000.

A conversation with an acknowledged high producer was most revealing. This salesman, although a great producer, had held a number of jobs in a relatively short period of time. Apparently, each time he reached the level where he was about to be promoted to sales manager, he would leave that company. While he made it clear to friends and coworkers that he aspired to be a manager, he never allowed himself to accept that position. He seemed afraid of the responsibility.

The former schoolteacher and the high producer, both shying away from responsibility, exhibited symptoms typical of those suffering from fear of success.

We have all either experienced the fear of success ourselves, or have met individuals who are victims of this "disease." Our society is filled with people who quit college when they were four units short of a degree, runners who dropped out of the race a few feet from the finish line, and playwrights who disappeared on opening night.

The fear of success usually stems from our youth and the messages implanted by our parents. When I was eight years old, I spent an entire day building a wooden go-cart. It was ugly at best, but, I thought it looked like a Formula 1 racer. When I showed it to my father, he promptly said, "When you get older, I'll show you how to build a good one." Heartbreak! My father failed to give me the praise and encouragement I needed to possess a feeling of accomplishment for all my work and effort. The sense of success I desired from building (what was to me) a sleek, fast go-cart suddenly didn't seem all that important.

## CONFLICTING MESSAGES

As children, we may have been programmed to feel guilty about attaining success. Part of that programming may have come from mixed messages from our parents. Did you ever hear these contradictory statements when you were growing up? *"You're too smart for your own good (but you had better bring home a good report card). Don't be a show off (but you'd better be a stand-out if you want to get ahead). Money is the root of all evil (but get out there, kid, and earn those bucks)."* This kind of negative criticism, coupled with conflicting messages and the expectations we feel, frequently causes confusion and a feeling of "even if I succeed, it's not good enough."

The roots of our fear of success could indeed stem from our upbringing. Probably, most of our parents were middle-class people who raised us with the belief systems and attitudes that are typical of that socio-economic status (SES for short). As long as we stay within the set boundaries in which we were brought up, all is well. However, as soon as we move beyond our SES limits because of our successes, we may begin to experience vague discomfort. The greater the distance from our childhood belief systems, the more pronounced that discomfort.

Success itself may not be the cause of our fear. Instead, it may be the trappings of success that make us feel uneasy. In *"The Beverly Hillbillies,"* a popular television series from the 1960s, a poverty-stricken family from Tennessee migrated to Beverly Hills as the result of striking it rich with an oil well. The character "Granny," constantly made demands on her son, "Jed," to go back to the hills of Tennessee. She was so uncomfortable with her newfound state of wealth that she turned her Beverly Hills mansion into a backhills poverty shack, whiskey still and all. Because her grandchildren, "Ellie May" and "Jethro" were, in a sense, still growing up and had not developed fixed notions about their proper status, they loved the new surroundings. They were learning to feel comfortable with this luxurious lifestyle and accepting it as a normal way of life.

## COMFORT LEVELS

Why is it that "the rich stay rich and the poor get poorer?" The answer lies in comfort levels. In the late 1970s, the Carter Administration poured millions of dollars into slum renovations, turning several New York city tenement buildings into clean, modern high-rise dwellings. These beautiful high rises quickly reverted to their earlier slum conditions as the families re-established their former comfort levels.

Social researchers have found that our family's financial status during our childhood is likely to be the level at which we feel most at ease as adults. When we experience the fear of success, we may be sabotaging our chances to make a higher income because of the sheer discomfort a change in lifestyle would bring.

Surprising as it may seem, most of us make within 10 to 20 percent of our best friend's income. What would happen if our income doubled this year? We'd be able to purchase a house in a more affluent area, buy new cars, and even have enough money to take an extended vacation. However, our friends probably wouldn't have the funds to share those exciting events with us. Going to a higher SES might entail making new friends and losing the old ones. Many of us would rather keep our old friends than try to cope with financial prosperity and its accompanying changes.

During a consulting project for a real estate company, I encountered a salesperson with *too* much business. An axiom of the consulting industry is that you can never have too much business. Once you get to your staff and resource capacity, you hire and train more people to take on the added work. Simple as this seems, the realtor's excuse for not attending an important conference was just that: "I've already got enough business. I don't need to attend." My response was, "Lee Iacocca doesn't have too much business and neither do you!"

What this person actually meant was, "I'm uncomfortable with my high success rate. I don't want to get in any deeper." She viewed her success as troublesome. For her, it might have been a disease rather than a blessing. Top salespeople in the real estate industry will often start up their own companies when they have more business than they can handle alone. But this woman seemed to fear the added responsibility of expanding her success.

## DO YOU DESERVE SUCCESS?

Our fear of success may come from feeling that we are not as deserving as others. In many cases, the fear of success stems from our admiration, respect or even awe of a boss, our parents or a mentor. In fact, we may feel, "They taught me everything I know. They're much more perceptive and intelligent than I could ever be." But, suddenly, we find ourselves making more money or achieving greater goals than those people we've admired for so long and we begin to question our own success.

The ultimate fear of success is suicide. Freddie Prinze, the great young comedian, probably committed suicide largely because of his discomfort with success. He spent hundreds of thousands of dollars on elaborate, expensive gifts for his parents, seemingly in an effort to relieve his guilt for being so successful.

Why did rock stars Elvis Presley and Janis Joplin, just at the time when they apparently had everything, self-destruct at the height of their careers and die of alleged drug over-doses? And, why did Richard Nixon commit political suicide by not destroying the White House tapes and thus avoid his own demise?

When we feel undeserving of success, we have a variety of methods for sabotaging ourselves. Do any of the following scenarios seem familiar to you?

You're playing golf and are about to putt on the 18th green. Three of your friends have already missed their putts. Last to putt, you realize that if you can sink this one-foot putt, you'll win that Michelob Light. You take a couple of practice swings, and then suddenly you get a flash. "Hey," you think, "My friends really should be winning. I've never beaten any of them before. Why am I ahead? I'm not as good at golf as they are." If you have no fear of success, why then, when you putt, does that ball go past the hole, all the way down to the clubhouse!

How about this court drama starring Bassett versus Evert-Lloyd? In 1984, on the women's tennis tour stop at Amelia Island, Florida, Chris Evert-Lloyd was pitted against Carling Bassett. Carling, Toronto's tennis darling, whose wealthy father was the late owner of the Tampa Bay Buc-caneers football team, was at the top of her game.

Playing superbly during the whole tournament, Carling now faced Chris Evert-Lloyd, the queen of the tennis court. True to her tournament form, Carling soundly trounced Chris in the first set, 6 to 3, and appeared to be about to defeat Chris in the second set of the best of three set match. At 5 to 2, Carling double-faulted her serve. She netted some easy shots, letting Chris back into the match. Chris Evert-Lloyd went on to win the next five games as well as the set. Evert-Lloyd defeated Bassett in what should have been an upset victory for Bassett.

Interviewed afterward, Carling admitted that she viewed Chris with respect and awe, and was not able to see herself beating this tennis great. Evert-Lloyd's image and reputation may have been more invincible than her strokes. Bassett beat herself. She sabotaged her excellent tennis form because she believed she didn't deserve to beat Evert-Lloyd. She feared success!

Carling Bassett is not the only pro tennis player to have experienced the fear of success. A few years ago, I had the opportunity to play a great tennis star named Yannick Noah. Noah had been discovered in Africa by Arthur Ashe, a renowned tennis player of the 1960s and 1970s. My chance to play against Noah came when I was in Cannes during the European Grand Prix.

Noah was a tremendously talented and gifted player. But after our match, he confided to me that he frequently had problems winning matches when he was way ahead. He told me the story of his trip to the United States to play tennis great Stan Smith.

They were in a five-set match. Noah was up two sets to love, 5 games to 1 in the third set. All he needed in order to win was three games. It should have been easy, but Noah began missing shot after shot, hitting balls out and double-faulting. Smith came back and won one game, then came back to win another, until eventually they tied the match, 5 to 5 in the final set.

Noah told me he felt extreme anxiety and fear. He felt upset at himself that he wasn't playing better, but he realized Stan Smith was winning only because he himself was "choking." Smith went on to beat Noah 7 to 5 in the fifth set.

What Noah described was really a fear of success. He believed that because he didn't have the level of experience of Stan Smith, he had no business out there with a player of Smith's caliber. Psychologically, Yannick Noah understood that he was good, but he feared Smith's reputation much more than he feared Smith's ability that day on the court.

In professional golf tournaments, the same thing often happens. A fairly easy putt is missed; a drive goes into the nearest pond or sand trap. Some of the best players can't seem to play well, or fail to keep their lead when they are ahead. This isn't just choking, or simply a lack of concentration. It actually stems from feeling self-conscious and anxious about doing so well. Our fear of success may come from feeling overly respectful of a job, or out of a mistaken idea that things should be a lot more difficult than they seem.

## PERFORMANCE PLATEAUS

When we experience the fear of success, we often find that we have reached a performance plateau. We may have worked long and hard to increase our productivity, but when we reach performance plateaus, we might find that we no longer seem to grow and improve as fast as we once did. Even though we might have loved what we were doing six months ago, our interest and enthusiasm about our jobs begin to diminish.

Fear-of-success sufferers often try to avoid the discomfort of success through tactics such as procrastination. In fact, even though fear-of-success sufferers know they should be working, they sometimes will take four to six weeks off, twice a year. All of us tend to have plateaus of productivity for a time. But when we reach performance plateaus, we may find that we do not grow and improve nearly as rapidly as our experience levels would predict.

An insurance agent once told me he was having problems with complacency. He was not achieving as much as he once did. In fact, he was not as motivated about his job as he had been in the past. He also said that he took about three months off during the year, and he only worked four to five hours a day. When I asked him why he didn't work harder, he said he really didn't know the answer.

I dug deeper and found that he was making $30,000 a year. But he had so much talent and so much drive, I was surprised he wasn't making $100,000 or more. He said that his father was a teacher in a local school district. He respected his father immensely. But his father was only making $25,000 per year. The father sometimes put in eighteen hours per day, read constantly, and worked hard to support his family.

The son felt guilty that he was making more money than his father did. He only had a high school education, while his father had a master's degree. The son, the insurance agent, felt it wasn't right to be making more money than his father.

To deal with his fear of success, the agent spoke to his father. He found that his father really enjoyed his job. He also realized that money was not an indication of worth or respect. The insurance agent tackled his fear of success head-on, and proceeded to double his income within two months. He now makes $100,000 a year and is growing as rapidly as you would expect of a hard-working, talented insurance agent.

## PEER PRESSURE

Fear of success also results from the pressures our friends put on us. As I suggested earlier, most of us make within 10 to 20 percent of our best friend's income. This can have a devastating impact on our productivity and success, because if we make substantially more than our friends, then we have greater freedom than they do. They aren't able to keep up with us. They don't have the same cars or the same houses. They aren't able to take the same vacations. People with more money try to find friends with equal resources, and those with less money do the same.

I saw this happen early in my life. A year out of college, a friend's sales business really took off. He was in the computer industry and was a top producer. The rest of us were just getting our business feet wet. I was gaining experience as a stockbroker, and the others were in management training jobs.

Gradually, the computer sales broker became more and more successful. We saw less and less of him, but we all admired his gains. He had a Porsche, a boat, and even a small house. He often said that he missed us, but we just couldn't keep up. He wanted to go snow skiing every weekend; we couldn't even afford our own skis. He had a hot ski boat; we could barely afford the gas for it.

He footed the bill for us a lot of the time, but we all felt awkward taking his charity. Suddenly his production sank. His success dwindled. Surprisingly, his setbacks didn't seem to phase him. We saw more of him after that, and learned that because of his dwindling income, he had to sell his boat and Porsche.

One night, while we were socializing, I asked him why he had let it all go. He said he didn't think it was worth all the effort. He missed his friends. What really happened was that success brought on too much change. The discomfort of losing friends was not worth the added benefits of more money. He decided to keep his less-monied friends and give up some of his success.

Friends are hard to find and even harder to keep. When your income goes up drastically, much more than what your friends make, you tend to feel stress. Your interests may change. You might want to be with other people in your income bracket. This can put an incredible amount of pressure on you. You may start feeling depressed and spend less time with friends. Or, you may feel classic stress symptoms such as loneliness, lethargy, and lack of motivation. If this is what success brings, you may not want it.


## WOMEN'S FEARS

Sales managers who employ women as salespeople often witness fear of success in them. I have worked with Mary Kay Cosmetics, a firm employing 100,000 female salespeople in the United States. A sales director for the company will recruit highly successful saleswomen and pay them on a commission basis. These saleswoman often will do so well that they quickly outpace the income level of their husbands. All too often, the male not only resents his wife working away from home in the evening, but is uncomfortable when her income exceeds his.

A saleswoman in Calgary, Canada told me that her husband constantly ridiculed her success as a salesperson. He seemed to feel that his masculinity was undermined by her great success. To avoid his barbs, she chose to keep her income level slightly below his. This was a very conscious, albeit unfortunate, fear of success consequence.

## OVERCOMING FEAR OF SUCCESS

But there are ways to welcome success and to overcome the fears that have been discussed. Here are three techniques to help overcome fear of success. Because the fear of success primarily entails feelings of guilt, in order to conquer the fear of success we must convince ourselves that we *deserve* to have wonderful achievements, that each of us is worthy of the success we desire.

First, we all give ourselves conflicting messages in our minds about how we should act and how successful we should become. Until these messages are changed and we make it O.K. to succeed, we'll continue to sabotage our own efforts. To help overcome those conflicting messages, list 10 reasons why you deserve to make more than $200,000 a year, drive a new Porsche, buy a new house or achieve your goals. Do it now!

Second, think of three things that you may be doing to avoid achievement. These avoidance tendencies could be procrastination, poor planning, no personal or business goals, or even refusing to implement new techniques and ideas, when you logically know they may help you to succeed. It's important to write down and possibly discuss these avoidance tendencies with your spouse or a friend in an effort to uncover possible success-sabotaging behavior.

Third, write down at least one accomplishment at the end of each day. In the evening, reward yourself for that success by eating your favorite dessert or watching that special television program, or by reading a favorite book or magazine. Be sure that you don't deprive yourself of your reward. Achievement may be it's own reward.

A financial planner in Michigan used a similar technique for 6 weeks to deal with his fear of success. His annual income went from $50,000 to $150,000 during those weeks. Last December, he bought a new Mercedes and is truly enjoying every day of his planned success.

While other methods may be useful, these three techniques will certainly give you a good starting point to help you deal with your own fear of success.

Not every one fears success. Most of us have a basic desire to be successful, and our society puts a premium on the value of success. But if your childhood experiences are marked by sibling rivalry, a lack of parental approval, negative criticism, and/or conflicting messages, you may fear success.

So, ask yourself the question, "Am I doing everything I can to achieve my dreams right now, or do I fear success?"

In the next chapter, we shall examine ways of motivating yourself permanently in order to achieve (and maintain) your desired success.

# PART 2

# MOTIVATING YOURSELF – PERMANENTLY

It is the third time Dennis M. has tried to book an appointment with a successful business owner. Even after an introductory referral letter, the owner has not returned Dennis's phone calls. Dennis wonders if he is getting through. He will give up after one more call.

Mark W. has heard that if one wants referrals, one must ask for them. So on his next appointment he does just that, but the prospect can't think of anyone offhand. The next day, Mark's manager asks why he is making cold calls. His reply is that he gets the best results with this method. His manager knows better. Following frequent discussions, Mark still refuses to work from referrals.

Susan S., with only six months experience, just closed a small and remarkably successful sale. Ecstatic, she goes back to her office and starts prospecting for more business. She thinks the opportunities are just lying out there waiting to be picked up off the ground. She's making more money than all her friends. She loves the feeling she gets from being successful.

## CAUSE AND EFFECT

A laboratory rat frantically presses a little red lever 200 times a minute in order to earn a few pellets of food. A driver receives a twenty five dollar ticket for parking too long in a ten minute waiting zone, and quickly learns to pay attention to his watch while his car is parked at a meter. In a Las Vegas casino, a woman on a one-week hard-earned vacation sits on an uncomfortable stool day after day, from sunup to sundown, feeding quarters into a slot machine.

What do these scenarios have in common? They all illustrate a basic tenet of human behavior called the *law of cause and effect*. That is, we tend to engage in behaviors that bring us rewards, and avoid those which result in punishment. This very obvious principle is part of a psychological science called behavior modification or "conditioning." For several years now, behavior modification techniques have helped producers increase their sales by as much as 310 percent within six weeks.

While attending a recent management association gathering, a manager described his favorite motivational tool. He called it his ".45 caliber test." He would hold an imaginary gun up to a low producer's head and say, "If I held a gun up to your head right now, would you make ten prospecting calls?" If the salesperson said no, the manager would pull the trigger. I kept thinking how many producers he would lose if he had a real gun. Is there some other way to stay consistently motivated?

Over the years, I have asked some of the most successful salespeople in the country how they stay so productive. In almost every case, they work toward daily (even hourly) goals. But, what I was most surprised to hear was that they give themselves frequent small rewards for achieving each objective. A big hitter in Philadelphia named Jay said he went to the driving range every afternoon after he saw at least three prospects. If he didn't achieve his goal, he was disciplined enough not to hit golf balls that day, even though it would be both enjoyable as well as a stress release.

Another producer, in Chicago, didn't eat lunch until he had

made at least five referral phone calls before noon. Do you think he lost a lot of weight? He dropped three pounds the first week and hasn't missed a meal since.

## CONSISTENT ACTIVITY

Why are strategies like this effective? Are these people just naturally disciplined? No. They have simply learned that what makes Johnny run now, may not make Johnny run later. Salespeople fail, not because of lack of selling ability, but rather from a lack of consistent activity. When I was a professional tennis player, I practiced my favorite serve, the 138-mile-an-hour flat serve. I bragged to my coach that I could burn a hole in my opponent's racket at ninety feet. He said, "I don't care if you can hit a ball through concrete, I want consistency!" These successful producers are not the ones who prospect furiously only on Monday. Rather they are the daily goal setters who develop and maintain persistent activity.

## IMMEDIATE REWARDS

Craig B. was experiencing a familiar problem. He was doing too little prospecting. He was great at setting goals, but he didn't seem to be able to reach them. He wanted a 500 SEL Mercedes, $150,000 net income per year and a vacation house at a lake resort. He even set time deadlines for each objective. What he failed to realize was that his goals were too far away to keep him motivated on a consistent basis. Sure he had a picture of the 500 SEL mounted on his office wall, but looking at it didn't change his level of activity. The only change was in his level of frustration. His self-esteem was disintegrating due to his inability to achieve the goals he had set for himself. Craig had two chances for arriving at his goals by the deadlines he had set – little and none. Unless he could restructure his reward system, he had almost no opportunity for success.

Rewards come in two flavors, immediate and deferred (long term). The more immediate the reward, the greater the effect it has on behavior. The longer the reward is deferred, the less influence it has on immediate behavior.

As graduate students, we tried to determine just how hard a pigeon would work to get a food pellet. By pressing a green lever, the bird would earn either an immediate or deferred reward. We discovered that if the pellet didn't fall down the chute quickly enough after the lever was pressed, the pigeon would not link the food to a reward for pressing the lever. In fact, when the food was delayed in falling into the cage, the bird would simply wait by the chute for the next pellet, ignoring the green lever. Many salespeople are like this pigeon; they wait by the telephone, expecting it to ring. However, if the pigeon received its reward immediately upon pressing the lever, it would peck the paint off the lever in an effort to keep the pellets coming.

## REWARDING YOURSELF

I asked Craig what he really enjoyed in life. He said reading was particularly satisfying to him. Fine music, a cigar, and a good book in the evening were heaven. He also enjoyed his share of favorite TV programs, and was partial to weekend golf. Next, I asked about activities he did during the day that he really enjoyed. He liked to have a cup of coffee in the morning, and read the *Wall Street Journal* at work. During his mid-morning break he enjoyed a soft drink and a doughnut. Since his activity goals were to make five referral calls per day, I made a deal with him. Every time he placed a call, he earned the right to take a sip of his soft drink. Only after he had made five calls could he have the doughnut. As you may have guessed, Craig became sensitive to the fact that he couldn't have his doughnut until he earned it. He was quick to relate his activity goals to immediate rewards. He told me that after a week, he looked forward to the reward of consuming the doughnut. His "pellet" had taken on a special meaning. He no longer had to make the association between prospecting and a deferred reward of income dollars each month, or company recognition each year.

Do immediate rewards work? You bet! When I played professional tennis in Europe, I found myself in a heated match with the famed tennis player, Ilie Nastase. Nastase, an emotional competitor, had an interesting way of immediately rewarding himself for winning difficult points. After a point, he would walk to the sideline and take a sip of Coke. Obviously, this was disruptive to the continuity of play, but the rules stated that he was allowed thirty seconds in between points before he had to start play. He found it self-motivational to use that time for reinforcement.

## SYSTEMATIC APPROXIMATION

A friend and I were attending a conference where we heard a dynamic motivational speaker. We were so charged up, both of us felt like running outside the meeting room and selling cars to people in the parking lot. My friend assured me he would double his business over the next year. A week later, I asked him about his progress. He said the first three days he had doubled his activity. The next three days he gradually regressed back to his previous effort level. What he failed to realize was that people don't change – they only make gradual modifications to existing behavior. I made him promise to increase his activity slowly over four weeks instead of four days, using a system of immediate rewards. Every two days he would increase his prospecting activity by one call. This not only prevented burnout, but also gave him time to adapt to a change in his behavior patterns.

When a psychologist treats an acrophobic (one who fears heights), he doesn't take the patient to the top of the Sears Tower and say, "Look at that view." Initially, they walk up to, but not into, the elevator. The second day, he takes the patient into the elevator, up to the next floor and back down. Each day they progress to a higher level in the elevator so that the patient has a chance to adapt to the fear, and more importantly, to the success he experiences during the process. Eventually, the patient is able to cope with the fear and enjoy being catapulted in elevators to high places without anxiety. This same technique of experiencing change slowly may be used to increase sales production. Experiencing change quickly is too much of a shock.

## THE PARTNERSHIP SYSTEM

Unfortunately, few of us stick to New Year's resolutions for more than a couple of weeks after January 1. We usually need help from an outsider to keep us honest. A "success partner" can be the key to maintaining resolutions all year. If you enlist the help of an associate or friend to keep you on track, you won't have to worry about maintaining your will power.

One producer I worked with gave a business associate (his success partner) a check for $100. This "promise deposit" was to be cashed by the partner under only two circumstances. The producer would forfeit his $100 if he did not achieve his daily goals, and *if he failed to reward himself*. The focus here is on the activity leading up to production rather than on the sale itself. At the end of the day, the agent and his partner would chat for five minutes to determine whether or not he had actually taken that sip of coffee or read that favorite book the evening before. If he missed taking his rewards, he would lose the $100.

Rewards are the most important part of your self-esteem support system. By rewarding and reinforcing yourself for at least four weeks, you will be able to dramatically increase your overall sales production. The success and enjoyment that result from modifying your own behavior then become the greatest motivators of all.

These simple concepts have resulted in amazing sales increases with numerous producers. One salesperson even increased his overall activity and sales by 356 percent within six weeks. Surprisingly, after the six weeks, he reportedly was not working any harder than at the onset of his program. He had learned the secret of creating his own success; self-motivation reinforced by immediate reward.

So, use immediate rewards and increase your activity slowly and surely. Enlist the support of a success partner to encourage you along the way. *You deserve more success!*

Motivation to achieve your goals can sometimes be hampered by a psychological malady known as *call reluctance*. We shall address this problem and offer techniques for overcoming it in the next chapter.

# PART 3

## OVERCOMING CALL RELUCTANCE

Don prides himself on being thorough. Even though he thinks of himself as a pro, he'd like his sales production to be a little higher. He's tired of watching new producers out perform him. It's obvious to him that they really don't know enough about their products. He, on the other hand, is always prepared and knows exactly what to say. The problem is, he doesn't say it often enough. He'd rather spend time analyzing than acting.

Bob considers himself successful. He is image conscious and knows how to act. After all, prospects like to deal with style and class. Bob believes he has to be the best salesperson around or he is nothing at all. His self-image is tightly woven into his behavior. He doesn't prospect much because he feels it is beneath him. To avoid the risk of humiliation or loss of self-perceived status, he instead dedicates much of his time to industry organizations and professional groups. He rationalizes that networking is better than prospecting. He would rather let others refer prospects to him through word of mouth. Unfortunately, this technique has never paid off for him. But at least it is better than exposing himself to prospects who don't know who he is.

Jennifer enjoys selling. She likes helping people solve their problems. She realizes that selling, while extremely profitable, can also be uncomfortable. She doesn't like to prospect from referrals or make cold calls. She is afraid of being thought of as pushy and intrusive. She frequently apologizes to prospects for interrupting them. She hesitates to pick up the telephone and start dialing, waiting for the "right time" to call. Jennifer realizes she doesn't make a lot of calls, but she is unwilling to take the risk of appearing too forward.

## IDENTIFYING CALL RELUCTANCE

Are you identifying with any of these people? They all possess a self-sabotaging psychological malady described as *call reluctance*. If your prospecting activity is too low, you may have call reluctance. To qualify, you must also possess goals and the motivation to achieve those goals. Unfortunately, you find it emotionally difficult to make yourself prospect, and thereby achieve those goals.

According to sales researchers Dudley and Goodson in their book, *Call Reluctance*, over 40 percent of the salespeople questioned report experiencing severe bouts of call reluctance that nearly ended their careers. Most managers agree it is the main reason many new salespeople fail, but few comprehend the impact it can have on more experienced producers, causing them to become complacent about searching for new business.

Recently, I received a letter from an attorney who had been in business for over ten years. I am on friendly terms with him since we see each other every week at our church Sunday school class. He knows me well enough to call on the telephone, but instead he sent me a four-page boilerplate prospecting letter. It must have taken him at least half an hour to dictate, not to mention the time his secretary took to type it. The letter described his corporate philosophy as well as his recommendations concerning my estate plan. It was so impersonal that I erased my name and scratched in "Dear Occupant," and then showed it to my wife. She thought it was a joke, and we promptly tossed it into the trash. This type of technique may work as a cold entry, but it indicated call reluctance to me.

The first step in dealing with call reluctance is recognizing specifically what it is and how it affects you. While there seem to be many types of call reluctance, four stand out as the most common: analytic, image-conscious, position-acceptance, and fear of intrusion.

## TYPES OF CALL RELUCTANCE
### *The Analytic Reluctant*

The *analytic* type of call reluctance occurs in salespeople who are overly sensitive about being swept away by their emotions. Afraid to show their true feelings, they preoccupy themselves in highly technical matters. *Analytics* keep their feelings in the deep freeze, fearing rejection if they reveal themselves. They over analyze and under act, appearing reserved and self-restrained in interpersonal conversations. When giving sales presentations, they tend to stress information while neglecting relationships. They sometimes even seem cynical about the value of interpersonal relations and the need for people skills.

When I was a stockbroker, I knew an *analytic* type named Ken. He had been with the firm for about five years, and was very knowledgeable about the stockmarket. In between my daily load of more than 150 cold calls per day, I would pop into his office for inspiration and advice. I would often see him looking over a stock performance history or working on one of his computer-based stock illustrations. I was shocked to learn that out of the fifteen or so producers, he was in the bottom 25 percent. Ken possessed the *analytic* call reluctance style. He tried to avoid making phone calls by preoccupying himself with computers and technical illustrations. He rationalized, at least unconsciously, that, "I'm going to keep

35

myself busy. If I don't make phone calls, that's okay. If people call me, that's wonderful. But I'm at least going to prove how sharp I am by thoroughly learning my product and the technical aspects of my job." Ken was not as concerned with getting business as he was with being technically proficient.

This form of call reluctance often occurs in highly professional people. Often physicians have a built-in call reluctance, as do attorneys and dentists. Often psychologists would never dream of calling anybody on the telephone, especially on a referral. It is something that's "not done" with those of us who are "technical types." This is probably one of the reasons why engineers rarely become salespeople. They would rather spend their time analyzing and working with data than dealing with people. I once went to an entrepreneurial class where the professor said, "If you want to bring a product to the marketplace and sell it, you need to learn the philosophy of *"ready, fire, aim."* He was trying to say, "Get as ready as you can, and then go for it." Once you have introduced that product into the marketplace, correct it, streamline it, make it better, and then fire again. The worst thing to do is prepare yourself, and then try to aim for perfection to the point that you never fire. Granted, if your product is better than any other one on the market, people will beat a path to your door to get it. But your knowledge of the technical features of the product may be lost on the majority of your prospects. You will read often in this book that your prospects buy your trust first, and buy what you recommend to fulfill their needs, second.

There is a difference between a peddler and a professional salesperson. A peddler is that individual who tries to convince anybody he possibly can to purchase his product. In contrast, a professional salesperson aims to solve concerns and resolve problems. He matches his product or service with the prospect who needs it. He also makes every effort to discover their goals and objectives, and literally takes problems off their worry list. This means that he is a problem solver who makes money by prescribing solutions rather than by hawking his wares.

I recently bought an insurance policy from a salesperson who demonstrated excellent selling skills. He ferreted out my needs and wants by asking specific and pointed questions to uncover my goals. He spent the majority of the first interview in this probing phase. The balance of the time was spent giving suggestions to me that I could implement. At this meeting, he presented an outline of problem-solving ideas for me to review. In interviewing other salespeople, I met with an insurance agent who listened to me talk for three or four minutes, and immediately told me what he thought I needed. While they both probed, one actually tried to get inside my head to find out what I needed technically, from a product standpoint, as well as what I required, emotionally, to solve my problems.

### The Image-Conscious Type

The *image-conscious* type of call reluctance is prevalent in those salespeople who try to overcome self-confidence and self-esteem insecurities by making a show of the trappings of success. They invest heavily in the appearances of wealth and achievement. Ostentatious in their displays of success, these types maintain a constant vigilance against any threat to their advertised respect and worth. In an effort to impress others, they often concentrate their energies on showy if not difficult sales. At times lacking qualifications or experience, they nevertheless work on endeavors with a low probability of success, believing these infrequent deals are compatible with their perceived professional image. Prospecting is beneath them and is seen as just plain undignified.

A salesperson I know fits this mold. He wears so much gold jewelry he looks like an executive version of Mr. T. He employs flunkies to make cold calls for him, due to what he claims is his lack of time. His production is low because he is still "streamlining his operation." He has a condescending way of speaking softly that makes others uncomfortable. One gets the feeling he manages to close a few large sales per year (which he brags about), although his overall profit margin is barely enough to support his financial needs. He continues to avoid prospecting until he's financially forced back into it in order to create more business.

These kinds of salespeople have what I call the "Superman salesperson complex." They attempt to shortcut the sales process by skipping the all-important building blocks to success. They want to reach up, grab the golden ring at the top of the staircase, and make that big sale. They don't want to struggle in the trenches with other salespeople who gut it out. This can happen to those salespeople who have transferred to a new location or a new company. They may have spent several years paying their dues. Then suddenly, they are forced to start all over again. One individual I know, in Canada, moved from a large metropolitan location to a small city near the Pacific coast. Very successful in his previous location, he just couldn't seem to make himself start from scratch and prospect for business with his new company in this new location. He experienced an image-consciousness, self-esteem crisis which precluded him from getting in the trenches and developing business from the bottom up. He didn't see himself as one who needed to start from the beginning.

## Position Acceptance Type

Call reluctance, with regard to *position acceptance*, occurs when an individual is embarrassed or apologetic in the role of salesperson. There is often a suppressed sense of dedication and zeal because this job or position is not considered professionally impressive. Such individuals sense that they are a disappointment to some significant person in their life such as a family member.

Such producers may suffer periods of job-related depression while pretending to be committed to their positions. They never fully believe the job will ever become a career. They may not believe that sales, or at least this type of sales, is valid or worthwhile.

I speak frequently to organizations populated by CPAs, MBAs or others who feel sales is not a career for those with "smarts." At one such meeting a new insurance agent showed me his card. Linked with a major life insurance company, he had been in the field only about eighteen months. Instead of reading "insurance agent," the card introduced him as, "John Smith, Investment Advisor." I asked him if he sold securities. He said, "Not really. I actually sell insurance products." He probably didn't realize that he was exhibiting *position reluctance*.

But *position reluctance* is inherent in individuals other than salespeople. The list of professionals who experience this type of call reluctance includes financial planners, dentists, attorneys, and other educated individuals. Some of these people think that selling is beneath them. Selling is for the uneducated, not for them. Salespeople are peddlers. They're hucksters, they're pitchmen. This *position acceptance* call reluctant type sees himself, not as a lowly salesperson, but as someone who provides a technical service. Unfortunately, those individuals who provide technical services are not ordinarily the individuals who get paid the highest amount of money. They're employed by managers who are literally put in business by the salesmen who spend their time digging up the business.

This *position acceptance* type of call reluctance is one that I had to deal with in my own personal career. After I received my Ph.D., I suddenly realized the only way I would be able to develop business was to get out and make phone calls. Since I wanted to consult to major companies in helping their salespeople achieve greater production, my only hope was to speak at various conferences and seminars in addition to making prospecting telephone calls. It was up to me to develop those speaking engagements, as well as to create more business. However, I had a great deal of difficulty seeing myself, a Ph.D., making prospecting telephone calls. My colleagues would not dream of engaging in such promotional activities. They simply would put an ad in the Yellow Pages or network with other professionals, hoping that they would refer business to them. I didn't want to wait that long. I immediately started making telephone calls at the rate of ten per day. I obviously received a great deal of business. Still, I felt guilty making those phone calls. Somehow, it didn't seem ethical. My college professors had drummed into me that Ph.D.'s are dignified professionals, not "phony flamboyant salespeople." In my case, I had to get over the image of a huckster and instead give myself an attitude of a competent salesperson who provides a service useful to others. Nothing happens until something is sold.

## Fear of Intrusion Type

The *fear of intrusion* types are those who don't want to be considered "pushy" or too aggressive. These people are unwilling to be assertive in prospecting for new business. They frequently lose control of the conversation or appointment, demonstrating an unwillingness to keep the prospect focused on the purpose of their call; that is, if they do actually prospect. They are overly concerned about the needs and desires of other people. A fear of intrusion type salesperson may postpone making a prospecting call because he is waiting for the right time. He may want an assurance that the prospect wants to talk with him. Unfortunately, the salesperson is rarely able to match the right time with the right person in the right place to prospect perfectly. He often makes calls to his referrals rather than to prospects, avoiding contact with prospects.

These people frequently accept a prospect's objections too quickly and have trouble closing as well. They may view highly aggressive salespeople as unprofessional. While they are warm and sociable, they often let the needs of others take precedence over their own objectives.

I spent a few hours with a new salesperson observing her prospecting skills. She was excited about dealing with people on the telephone, but was a little intimidated by gruff prospects. I listened to her approach. She said, "Hi, Mr. Prospect, my name is Irma Matthews. I'm with Prime Investment Company. Did I interrupt anything? Were you busy? If so, I could call back later." That's all I needed to hear. I quickly zeroed in on her lack of assertiveness. She said she had trouble believing that what she wanted to talk about was as important as what the prospect was doing when she called.

Often *fear of intrusion* types are those who have a self-esteem problem. They are so focused on what other people think of them that they lose sight of what they are trying to accomplish. Not only are these individuals concerned with the needs and desires of other people, but they take their prospect's resistance too seriously. The *fear of intrusion* type possibly has what is known as a primary fear of selling. Many of us suffer from this. We don't like to get rejected. We don't enjoy getting a hard time, or experiencing resistance from prospects. But salespeople with this primary fear may take even the slightest criticism personally. If a prospect says something like, "I'm not sure I can use that," the *fear of intrusion* type salesperson might feel self-conscious, and immediately withdraw without discovering what the objection actually means. They may cave in to the objection too rapidly. These people sometimes appear apologetic for making telephone calls or even calling on prospects face-to-face.

A salesperson who was having problems with his production asked me to observe him while he was closing a prospect. After much explanation, he eventually got around to the close. He said, "Gee, does this system sound like one you can use?"

The prospect said, "Well, I guess so." The salesman then said, "Are you sure this is right for you?" He actually talked himself right out of the sale by over analyzing his prospect's intentions. He was so afraid of creating conflict with his prospect that he eventually lost the sale. The fatal error occurred when the salesperson caused the prospect to feel equally self-conscious and unsure of his decision.

## DEALING WITH CALL RELUCTANCE

Albert Ellis, Ph.D., a leader in rational emotive therapy, has an interesting way of dealing with phobics. He believes that human beings engage in a series of irrational thoughts to support a fear, whether it is a fear of heights or a fear of asking a prospect to buy a product or service. Those irrational mental processes reinforce our own negative self-image. Ellis believes that if we can interrupt and replace our internal dialogue of thought patterns, we can allow ourselves to release the extra mental baggage we carry.

For example, a salesman might pick up a telephone and internally worry, "This referral really isn't a very good prospect. I've dealt with these types before. They're rude and curt. I really don't think now is a good time to call. Executives like this always get lots of calls from salespeople in the morning. I think I'll wait until the afternoon when things slow down for him."

## FOUR EASY STEPS

Use these four steps the next time you have a bout of call reluctance: 1) observe; 2) pattern-interrupt; 3) substitute; and 4) reward.

## Observe

First, *observe* yourself experiencing call reluctance. Pay careful attention to what you are going through. Chances are you have let your self-sabotaging irrational thoughts drag your personal esteem through the mud. Detach yourself, for once, from your emotions and simply be an observer instead of a participant. You are probably thinking, "Hey Kerry, detaching myself from my emotions is a fairly difficult thing to do. How am I supposed to do that?" One simple method for effecting a phobia cure is a concept developed through neurolinguistic programming. Using this therapy, a phobia sufferer watches himself in a mental movie, imagining himself on the screen. He sees himself experiencing the fear and all that's entailed with it. He is able to feel the heart palpitations, the perspiration, and the shakes caused by anxiety. When he sees this happening, he is better able to deal with the uncomfortable emotions that brought on the fear in the first place. If you can imagine yourself as the central character on the movie screen, experiencing your heart pounding, the perspiration, and the dread you feel on the telephone, you will be able to aid yourself in recognizing the symptoms you are going through during call reluctance episodes. After you have run your movie, the next step is to engage in the pattern-interrupt and reward phases. From now on, when you start feeling those emotions, detach yourself by watching your mental movie.

A salesperson reported testing this method. As he was about to follow up on a referral lead, he started to feel call reluctance panic. His palms became moist, his heart palpitated, and he became aware of his irrational mental dialogue. "I really don't want to make this call. I feel myself becoming afraid of the telephone. If the prospect thinks I am intruding on his time, what will I say? He won't want to spend his time talking with me because he'll know I'm new at this type of call. He'll probably recognize how scared I am of talking with him." The salesperson saw how his fears were influencing his logical thought.

## Pattern-interrupt

The second step is to *interrupt*. By recognizing when the irrational thought patterns of call reluctance set in, you can interrupt yourself. Irrational thoughts seem to feed on themselves in a compounding way, like a snowball rolling down a hill. When next you become aware that those patterns have surfaced, immediately do something physical. Stand up and walk around your office. Say out loud what you are thinking internally. One effective way to interrupt the pattern is to cause yourself quick physical discomfort. Wear a rubberband around your wrist. When you become self-sabotaging, snap the rubberband. The sting will break the cycle.

## Substitute

Third, immediately *substitute* a positive experience to replace the negative one. In the book, *Take Charge* by William Redd and William Sleator, the authors discovered that negative messages are our own worst enemy. If you have been selling for even a few weeks, you have probably made at least one successful telephone call. You also probably recall how easy it seemed at the time, and how good you felt during and after the conversation. Get a 3 X 5 card, write down that prospect's name, and record every detail of how you felt during and after that call.

## Reward

Finally, after every call, give yourself an immediate *reward*. Whether your were able to speak to your prospect or not, reward yourself. A reward can be anything from a sip of coffee to calling your spouse, or even popping a breath mint into your mouth. A reward will reinforce the telephone call and increase the likelihood that you will make another call.

One financial planner with the fear of intrusion reported his success using this four-step technique. He realized he felt almost apologetic for making certain prospecting telephone calls. His heart would palpitate and beads of sweat would form on his forehead as he started to dial the phone number. When he finally observed his own phobic reaction, he was able to interrupt himself with a rubberband snap and recall a past successful call. Then he started to make the previously dreaded calls, following each one with a sip of coffee as a reward. Not only did his level of anxiety decrease, he finally was able to increase his revenues on the telephone, and also call past referrals for appointments he had put off for months.

If you are good on the phone, you'll be light years ahead of your competition. When you learn to recognize what call reluctance is and do something about it, business will simply flow to you. Good luck and happy dialing!

Often, one's personality type will affect behavior and achievement. The next chapter offers help in identifying your behavorial characteristics.

# PART 4

# TYPE A/TYPE B BEHAVIOR: ARE YOU BURNING OUT?

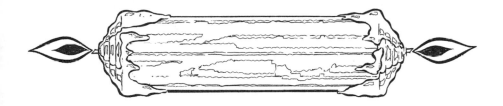

Have you ever considered your personality type? Have you noticed whether your behavior helps or hinders you in your efforts to achieve your goals? Is stress a major factor in your life, or do you roll with the punches?

## TEST FOR STRESS

Psychological research has identified behavioral characteristics that may contribute to your level of stress. Take the following test to determine how many apply to you. Do you:
1) Finish others' sentences before they do?
2) Move, walk, or eat quickly?
3) Prefer a summary instead of skimming or scanning a complete article?
4) Become upset in slow lines of traffic?
5) Generally feel impatient?

6) Find yourself disinterested or unaware of details?
7) Try to do two or more things at once?
8) Feel guilty if you relax or take a vacation?
9) Link your worth to quantitative tangibles like income, company growth, or number of employees?
10) Try to schedule more and more activities into less and less time?
11) Think about other things while talking to someone?
12) Exhibit nervous gestures like drumming your fingers or tapping your pen?
13) Continue to take on more and more responsibility?
14) Accentuate key words in ordinary speech when there is no reason to do so?
15) Work hurriedly even though deadlines are not pressing?

If you answered "yes" to ten or more of these characteristics, then consider yourself a Type A personality. Type A people run a higher risk of heart attack than Type B people. In fact, Type A's are twice as likely to contract heart disease as well as feel higher levels of both anxiety and depression. Is it time for you to start learning how to avoid being a Type A person?

Two cardiologists, Drs. Friedman and Rosenmann, wrote a book entitled, *Type A Behavior And Your Heart.* They discovered 20 percent of their stressed patients contracted 80 percent of all cases of heart disease. They also determined that these individuals had 70 percent more chance of contracting heart disease than other patients. They said that due to their personality characteristics, these people had a greater tendency to feel stress and have psychological and physical pain from that stress. The cardiologists called these people Type A's. These Type A patients were much more likely to decrease their life expectancy simply because of their personality characteristics.

It is fairly easy to spot a Type A unless it is you. A Type A person does not pay attention to self-help information. He rarely accepts advice from others because of his own vague and constant hostility towards them. If a Type A experiences symptoms of stress, he may visit a psychologist but will probably resist counseling.

A textbook example of a Type A is John, a highly successful, hard working, driving, respected salesman. He likes his work very much. Indeed, John is so proud of his sales achievements that he keeps constant reminders of his current production on his desk. He is continually trying to increase his sales volume by working harder and harder. He seems to spend more and more hours in the office. As if that wasn't enough, he uses a stop watch to track production, and often yells to his secretary, "We have $3^3/_4$ minutes left to complete this project." He also finds that his secretaries don't last long on the job. But when one leaves, John says, "I didn't really like her anyway."

John has trouble coping with traffic jams. He can't muster enough patience to wait in lines, even in fast food restaurants. He rarely has time to attend family gatherings. He claims he has too much to do. He tries to motivate newcomers in his company by appealing to their great desire to achieve. He makes every effort to set a good example by never complaining to his colleagues. But in private life, he unloads his gripes to his wife about how a customer or business associate upset him. He quite frankly admits feeling stressed, especially about things he cannot change. Recently he visited a doctor who told him that his blood pressure and cholesterol count were too high. The doctor recommended that he should watch his diet and learn to relax. It was easy for John to decrease his cholesterol level by cutting down on butter and eggs and other dairy products. But try to relax? Fat chance. To do nothing, or be engaged in what he considered "non-productive leisure" would be too uncomfortable to him. When John realized that he may have been putting too much stress on himself, he learned to exercise. He started jogging to keep his heart going but was unaware that his arteries were clogged from the long-time effects of cholesterol and chronic bombardment of hormonal secretions released by his constant anxiety. John's chances of leading a normal life and reaching a ripe old age are practically nil.

## CHARACTERISTICS OF TYPE A'S

Indepth examination has disclosed several behavioral characteristics common to Type A individuals. According to Friedman and Rosenmann, some of these traits include:

1) Moving and speaking quickly with vigor and even force.

2) The habit of interrupting others during a conversation. Type A's may even complete sentences instead of listening to others.

3) Trying to do more and more in less and less time. In spite of his efforts, he feels guilty for his lack of productivity.

4) Failing to enjoy the simple stuff of life. He ignores sunsets and quiet time as well as walks in the park or along the beach.

5) Feeling compelled to prove he is smarter, better, and infallible at all costs.

6) Possessing a need to say, "I told you so," or "If you would only have listened to me, you would never have had this problem."

7) General distrust of others. However, when questioned, he will deny having feelings of suspicion and distrust.

8) Appearing to be extroverted and independent on the outside, while actually introverted and dependent deep down. He may often brag about the extent of his accomplishments, believing that his facade of confidence and cockiness is vital to his business survival.

9) Being intensely driven. He feels a lack of self-worth unless he accomplishes something. This may be the biggest reason he acts the way he does.

10) Exhibiting extreme ambition to achieve at all costs. He may have an issue to prove that he is as good or better than others.

11) A competitive spirit in even minor tests. He has an intense desire to win a race, whether on the freeway or waiting

for a green light at a traffic signal.

12) Obsessive attention to time. This individual may glance at his watch every five minutes. In fact, if he is in a dentist's office and has to wait to see the dentist, he may look at his watch, approach the receptionist, and ask if he can use her phone to schedule his next appointment.

13) A quick, staccato voice pattern that is so rapid you have to listen extra hard to avoid being confused.


## BECOME A "TYPE B"

Type B's, on the other hand, react much differently in business than do Type A's. These top business managers and executives know they must develop Type B characteristics if they are to have profitable, long-lasting careers. Type B individuals examine their own behavior often to determine when and how they can change. They are sensitive to the needs of people around them. They are also more open and friendly, and often more cooperative than Type A's. Of course, they are not as time conscious, and yet they seem to be aware of the correct time. You will rarely find these individuals looking at their watches. Just as Type A's drive themselves to activity, their level of stress will also increase unless they learn to develop more Type B characteristics.

Sociologist and psychologist David Glass says A personalities would benefit greatly from making each work day as predictable as possible. These hyperactive types need to write down a daily plan in order to develop priorities that will help them stay organized, thereby decreasing stress. They must also determine the best way to complete a task, instead of concentrating on speed. They would do well to handle only one thing at a time. A great discipline for Type A's would be to find the longest line at the store or theater, and then wait in it as an exercise in patience. A Type A must realize that a whole person has more than a business side, and devotes time and energy to other facets of his life such as family and God. He must never forget the importance of fulfilling himself personally and spiritually.

We have listed the characteristics of Type A's. I am sure you can see whether you are a Type A person who is more apt to contract heart disease and chronic stress, or a Type B individual who copes well with stress.

Type A's may seem to be the ones who get the most accomplished. In reality, however, they work in spurts, putting out fires. Some argue that they start them as well. Type B's may be more productive in the long run. They certainly seem to enjoy life more. So instead of causing yourself Type A hypertension, anxiety, depression, and heart disease, why not use the prescribed techniques to become a Type B? Not only will you be more productive, you may have more zest for life and last longer, too!

In the next chapter we will discuss symptoms and solutions relating to stress.

# PART 5

# HOW TO STAMP OUT STRESS

John F. Kennedy's assassination shocked the United States. A mourning nation grieved the loss. A twenty-seven-year-old army captain led the funeral procession as John F. Kennedy's body was transported by a caisson of wagons. One week later, that same twenty-seven-year-old captain died of a massive heart attack.

A seventy-five-year-old man bet two dollars on a long shot at the race track. When his horse won, he became ecstatic at the prospect of winning $1,600. He was so overwhelmed, in fact, that just as he arrived at the window to collect his winnings, he collapsed and died.

What do these two victims have in common? One was old, one was young. One died during a period of national grief, the other feeling overwhelming joy. Yet both shared a common denominator; they both experienced deep change just prior to their death. Seventy percent of medical problems are stress-caused, according to many medical researchers. Yet only 2 percent of patients tell their physicians about their emotional problems.

## STRESS AND CHANGE

Stress is not simply the result of bad sales or a market downturn. Stress is truly the result of change, whether it is positive or negative. To be even more precise, the more unexpected the change in habits or environment, the greater the likelihood that stress will affect you. Stress is not just the chronic malady of the overburdened; it can also result in unexpected illness due to drastic change.

A life insurance agent friend of mine doubled his production in 1984. It shot up so fast, in fact, that he employed ten new administrative people to support him. He was able to spend more time with his family, and experienced great pride in his achievement. Yet in November of that year, he caught mononucleosis. Bedridden for three months, his business was near bankruptcy. Eight months later, his wife left him, taking with her their three-year-old son. Stress seemingly was a major factor in his setbacks. His life changed too quickly for both himself and his spouse. The result was illness and marital problems.

In the short term, the symptoms of stress seem obvious to spot. A prospect you are close to selling won't return your phone calls. You may even have a prospect who won't return necessary paperwork after you have spent many months selling him. You may even have home office employees who move so slowly they seem more like monolithic structures than alert human beings.

Your response to stress is fairly predictable, as are the stages of behavior you will go through during stressful situations. The following are four steps you will experience during stressful situations:
1) Alarm
2) Resistance
3) Adaptation
4) Fatigue

## STRESS SCENARIO

Here's a scenario explaining these four stages of stress. A

client of many years is approached by a competitor. He convinces your loyal customer that the life product you sold him is obsolete and a bad investment. Why not buy a cheaper security and put the savings into a higher paying fund? When you discover the transgression, you also experience shock and *alarm*. How could this happen. Why is the client so stupid to listen to people like that? Those dirty replacement artists!

The next stage is *resistance*. You may contemplate bombing your competitor's building, or at least slicing his tires. You may walk up and down the hallways of your office, complaining to everyone you see. You feel yourself tensing more and more as you talk about your situation. After writing letters to well-chosen recipients, you decide the best thing to do is call the client and explain to him how he was wronged.

Third, you start to *adapt*. You rationalize that it might be more work to pursue than it is worth. You may even contemplate ways of preventing replacement of policies in the future.

The final stage is *fatigue*. Even though you first learned of the replacement a few hours ago, your whole body feels like a twenty-ton truck ran over you. Every muscle aches. You're mentally exhausted and emotionally spent. The consistent theme in this example is that the more time you spend resisting the stressful situation, the more fatigued you will be in the end. Have you ever arm wrestled? While each competitor tries to pin the other's hand and arm onto the table, they will experience one common result. Each will be exhausted after the match. The more strenuously you resist the stress, the more fatigued you will become.

In the late 1970s in Linz, Austria, I competed against an Austrian hometown champion. "Boris," as he was called in those days, was favored to win the tournament. In fact, the tournament directors tried to insure his championship win by inserting him in the semi-finals without competing in the preliminary rounds like the rest of us. It was common, in those days, for an audience "draw" like this Austrian to receive money "under the table" to entice him to show up. This appearance stipend was often more money than the winner's purse. Boris won the first set. I was ahead 5 to 3 in the second set when Boris tossed the ball up to serve. But instead of serving the ball to me, he served his racquet. He threw his tennis racquet across the net, and it went whizzing over my head. My *alarm* stage set in. I felt shocked that this would actually happen. I then *resisted*. I ran over to the chair umpire and demanded Boris be ejected from the match. The tournament directors weren't about to expel an investment property as valuable as their champion. I then *adapted* by realizing my efforts at retribution were useless. I walked back onto the tennis court and stood ready to play. But I felt exhausted, as though I had already played a five-set match. I spent so much time resisting the situation that I *fatigued* my-self and was unable to play effectively throughout the rest of the match. Boris went on to win the second set 7 to 5 and take the match.

## TYPES OF STRESS

There are two distinctive types of stress, one called *Canon* and the other *Seyle*, named after the great Canadian endo-crinologist, Hans Seyle. The Canon or fight/flight response to stress was useful during prehistoric times at periods of phys-ical threat. If you were attacked by a saber-toothed tiger, Canon stress would help you climb a tree quicker than a cat.

### *CANON STRESS*

In fact, you've probably heard about the woman who lifted the front end of a car to free a child pinned underneath, or Olympic athletes who set world records turning in all-time personal best scores, times, and distances. During periods of physical threat, Canon stress saves lives, but except for these unusual examples, it serves to take lives. Physical symptoms of Cannon stress are:

1) *Muscle pain or illness.* Have you ever come home at the end of a bad day at the office feeling as if you'd been run over by a Sherman tank? You could have been suffering from Canon stress. Even though you may not have lifted more than a pencil, the constant tensing and relaxing of muscles can leave you feeling as if you had run a marathon.

2) *Tension headaches.* Unlike migraines, this type of headache is caused by the tensing of skull muscles. Often aspirin can help relieve this pain although relaxation techniques are more effective.

3) *Ulcers in the stomach lining.* Because the stomach muscles are also in tension, digestion continues in the form of acid release. The acidic content causes ulcerations in the stomach lining.

4) *High blood pressure.* Because of automatic tightening of muscles, even the capillaries are affected. Blood pressure is increased by blood being redirected away from the extremities toward the torso, putting pressure on the heart.

5) *Cancer.* I never understood the true magnitude of how cancer can be affected by stress until recently. In 1979, my mother, JoAnn Johnson, had a lung removed because of cancer, even though she had never smoked a pack of cigarettes in her whole life. In February of 1987, she collapsed in her home, paralyzed with a malignant brain tumor. I am grateful that the neurosurgeon was able to extract all of the cancerous tissue. She is recovering beautifully, regaining all of her thought processes. The neurosurgeon said, after the operation, that the cancer, which had been latent for twelve years, was activated because of stress. The cancer spread directly into her brain as a result of Canon-related stress.

Some of the psychological symptoms you may recognize are:

1) *Intractable fatigue.* This is a condition in which one is actu-

ally too tired to sleep. I sometimes find myself too exhausted to fall asleep after I have traveled through time zones. The exhaustion is so great it interferes with my ability to rest.

2) *Insomnia*. Because the muscles in the body are kept in such a state of tension, the body can't relax enough to fall asleep. Insomniacs often report being caught in a "Catch 22" cycle of stress. They become so afraid of not sleeping at night that their anxiety levels soar, causing even more severe insomnia. You may experience this during periods of pressure at work or at home.

3) *High irritability levels*. Bobby Knight, basketball coach for the Indiana Hoosiers, once threw a chair onto the court during a game because of a high irritability level due to tension.

4) *Lack of concentration*. If you have ever traveled, you have undoubtedly spent time sitting in an airport. Did you try to read or concentrate? During this high-stress time of waiting for a flight, it becomes difficult to concentrate or follow through on a thought.

5) *Acute anxiety*. The psychological discomfort caused by stress serves to stir up apprehension and anxiety, occasionally to the point of fear.

Your response to stress is really like a big balloon. The more pressure and change you are under, the more your stress balloon will inflate, causing you to develop these symptoms, and eventually perpetuating a major mental or physical catastrophe like a heart attack or stroke as well as mental disease.

The second type of stress, Selye stress, works in a different way. Also reacting to perceived change, this type of stress serves to effect problems with other systems in the body. Both Canon and Selye stress work on the presumption of a weak link. Every one of us has a weak link physically or mentally. This weakness is the first part to break, and because of this no two people will react to stress alike. Some may never have heart attacks, while others, like me, stay awake with insomnia while under stress.

## SELYE SYMPTOMS

Some Selye stress symptoms you may experience are:

1) *Migraine headaches.* Often feeling as though pain is wrapped around the head, or centered unilaterally in one area, these types of headaches cause more pain than simple headaches. They can result in flu-like symptoms. Once they begin, it becomes difficult to break the cycle of misery that sets in.

2) *Rash or skin eruptions.* You have undoubtedly seen people red-faced when upset. Others, like my wife, actually break out into a facial rash during stress. I usually know how much stress she's under by looking at her blotched skin.

3) *High vulnerability to illness.* Selye stress lowers the body's natural resistance to illness. If you have had the flu or a cold more than once this past year, you may be suffering from stress.

4) *Heart disease.* This is often due to coronary artery obstructions, causing damage to the heart itself.

5) *Gray hair.* Even though you've been using Grecian Formula for years, you may be surprised to learn that the pigment of hair, called melanin, actually is destroyed during stress, leaving hair a premature gray.

6) *Male pattern baldness.* This is obviously hereditary, but it also can be accelerated during periods of high stress. The smooth scalp muscles may actually constrict the hair follicles, causing the hair shaft to fall out more quickly.

The psychological symptoms of Selye stress are:

1) *Depression.* Defined psychologically as loss to oneself, depression can trigger periods of hopelessness and helplessness. Serious depression can lead to suicidal thoughts (the highest number of suicides in our society occur between the ages of seventeen and twenty-five years, the ages in which there is radical physical and emotional change). Over 70 percent of the adult population in America reports serious

depression at least once a year.

2) *Psychosis.* Many psychologists believe all of us possess latent psychotic tendencies. The line between normality and abnormality is a thin one. Stress-related pressures can push us across that line, causing ordinarily normal people to exhibit very unpredictable and unstable behavior.

## COPING WITH STRESS

Now that you've identified with a large number of these stress-related symptoms and are thoroughly unnerved, I'll list ways of dealing with stress. It is practically impossible to totally eradicate stress from your life. But, you can cope so well that you will cause your performance to improve rather than deteriorate, even under the most stressful conditions. It's not what happens to you that can result in further stress, it's how well you manage what happens to you, and your response to it.

### S.U.D.S.

The way to cope with stress is S.U.D.S. – drink lots of beer! Seriously, this acronym stands for Subjective Unit of Discomfort Scale. During periods of stress, you can actually measure your physical and psychological response in increments of 10, from 0 to 100. Each of these subjective units (0, 10, 20, etc.) also corresponds to symptoms you may have as a result.

A low-stress situation, such as having a relaxing drink as you are about to fall asleep in front of the fireplace, measures 0. High stress is 100. For example, you may feel high stress following a group of ninety-nine motorcycle-riding, chain-carrying, Hell's Angels on the freeway when your car horn gets stuck. This would quickly raise your S.U.D.S. level to 100! 

Here's a question for you. What level of stress on the

S.U.D.S. scale do you experience during the average day? In fact, what are your lowest and highest levels? 20? 40? 80?

If your stress level is generally higher than 45, you may suffer symptoms of burnout. If your S.U.D.S. level gets below 30, you may experience rustout. The following chart will give you a good idea of the symptoms you may experience.

## S.U.D.S.
### Subjective Unit of Discomfort Scale

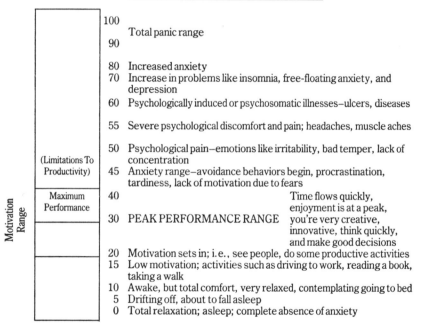

| | | |
|---|---|---|
| | 100 | |
| | | Total panic range |
| | 90 | |
| | 80 | Increased anxiety |
| | 70 | Increase in problems like insomnia, free-floating anxiety, and depression |
| | 60 | Psychologically induced or psychosomatic illnesses–ulcers, diseases |
| | 55 | Severe psychological discomfort and pain; headaches, muscle aches |
| (Limitations To | 50 | Psychological pain–emotions like irritability, bad temper, lack of concentration |
| Productivity) | 45 | Anxiety range–avoidance behaviors begin, procrastination, tardiness, lack of motivation due to fears |
| Maximum Performance | 40 | Time flows quickly, enjoyment is at a peak, |
| | 30 | PEAK PERFORMANCE RANGE  you're very creative, innovative, think quickly, and make good decisions |
| | 20 | Motivation sets in; i.e., see people, do some productive activities |
| | 15 | Low motivation; activities such as driving to work, reading a book, taking a walk |
| | 10 | Awake, but total comfort, very relaxed, contemplating going to bed |
| | 5 | Drifting off, about to fall asleep |
| | 0 | Total relaxation; asleep; complete absence of anxiety |

Motivation Range

If you can keep yourself between 30 and 45, you will stay in a "peak performance range." Everything will flow and you'll lose track of time. This is where you'll do your best work. When I play tennis, two hours feel like five minutes. When I'm prospecting for business, I enter this range when I start to enjoy the telephone calls. But if I let my discomfort rise above 45, I will perform more poorly in selling situations. The same is true if I decrease my discomfort below 30. You see, stress can actually help as well as hurt you.

## PROGRESSIVE RELAXATION

One extremely effective technique in bringing down your S.U.D.S. level is progressive relaxation. Nearly everybody who successfully copes with stress applies some form of relaxation technique to bring their body's response to stress into a manageable level. Many salespeople pay enormous amounts of money to be hooked up to a biofeedback machine in order to help them relax. The same technique I'm about to explain to you in this chapter, however, serves equally well in relieving symptoms and producing a more relaxed demeanor.

The first step in this simple procedure is to make sure you are seated in a comfortable position. Then, tense and relax your muscles as you inhale and exhale, mentally moving through every general area of your body, starting with your ankles and feet, and slowly moving all the way up to the muscles in your head. As you pause in each general area, tense for a period of three seconds while you inhale and exhale, then relax the muscles and release. After you've completed this step, imagine yourself at the top of a staircase with ten steps. Feel yourself inhaling and exhaling slowly with each step as you start from step ten and descend all the way down to step one, becoming more relaxed with every step. Thirdly, when you get to the bottom of the staircase, imagine yourself in a grassy meadow, beneath an oak tree. Hear the birds chirping in the tree, the wind blowing softly through the leaves. Leave yourself under the tree for five or ten minutes, and then take five steps back up the staircase to a more alert mode. If you do this every day for the next six or seven days, you will, in effect, be able to bring your body down to a fully relaxed, stress-free state.

Many people who have used this technique are able, after two weeks, to simply picture the forest and feel more relaxed. This is especially useful in meetings, or when you're face-to-face with a prospect who may give you a tough time.

## P.Q.R.S.

Another technique in dealing with the effects of stress is called the P.Q.R.S. technique. This technique is helpful in mentally coping with stressful situations. P stands for *prepare.* Because the definition of stress, as you recall, is unpredictable change, then preparing for a potentially stressful situation could help you cope with it. If you realize that tomorrow morning you will have a meeting with a difficult prospect, getting eight hours of sleep and eating a good meal may help you keep your stress at a manageable level. Also, make sure that as you prepare, you take a vitamin B complex of B1, B3, B6, and B12, and decrease your intake of coffee, tea, or other stimulants, especially during a day that you think a stressful event might occur.

Q is *question.* You know, now, that the four stages of stress are alarm, resist, adapt, and fatigue. If you resist stress or stressful situations, you will certainly feel more fatigued afterward. In other words, the effects of stress will be much more debilitating. So, question your response. Is it really worth getting upset over? Is it something that you want to make an issue of, knowing full well that the stress you receive from fighting that situation might not be worth the hassle? The price you pay may not be worth the benefit.

R is *relax.* Plan to spend five minutes out of every ninety minutes simply sitting in your office, walking yourself down the staircase and into the meadow, lying under the tree. Put yourself in that position for at least five minutes, and you'll find that your productivity will increase because you will think more clearly and concisely.

S is *solve.* It's not the elephants that get you, it's the mosquitoes. It's not the big things that you have the most trouble coping with, it's the small things. The little things that eat at you, little by little, every day, eventually cause your anxiety balloon to burst. But if, instead, you engage in a problem-solving campaign to make sure the little things don't defeat you, you will be able to cope with ease.

Use each of these techniques for the next two weeks. Use both the "progressive relaxation" as well as the "PQRS technique". Also, try to measure your stress on a daily (and even hourly) basis, by putting yourself on the S.U.D.S. scale at regular intervals. Using these techniques may not eradicate stress from your life, but they will certainly help you cope. They will not get rid of the situations that cause stress, but if you diligently and effectively use these techniques, you will help make stress work for you and increase production, rather than work against you and cause you distress and "dis-ease."

In the next section, "How to Get Inside Your Customer's Mind," we will discuss psychological techniques and methods hat can aid in increasing your productivity. The first of these, Subliminal Selling Skills, is addressed in the next chapter.

GAME STRATEGY

# 2

---

# HOW TO GET INSIDE YOUR CUSTOMER'S MIND

# PART 6

# SUBLIMINAL SELLING SKILLS

Do you realize you're being subliminally seduced almost every single day by almost every part of your outside business and personal environment? If you're thinking that subliminal seduction in advertising has been outlawed, you are right – to a certain extent. Fifteen years ago when the Coca-Cola Company flashed one frame of the logo, "Coke," on a motion picture screen, they found that Coke sales during the intermission increased. But popcorn and candy sales increased as well. When the government found out about the manipulative strategies of this company, they quickly outlawed the subliminal tactics – but only in the cinema. You are being seduced daily in many other ways as well.

## SUBLIMINAL SUGGESTIONS

Have you ever been to Las Vegas? Casino owners have known for a long time how to seduce you. They've known to decrease their lights to fairly hypnotic levels in order to entrance customers without entrapping them. They've also known not to put clocks or windows in their casinos, because without these, people are oblivious to the time and will stay in the casinos, gambling just a little bit longer. You will never play an isolated slot machine in Las Vegas. Six or more slot machines are placed together in rows. To insure that you will continue gambling even if the machine you're playing doesn't hit, you will hear the seductive sound of coins as all the other slot machines around you pay off. The logic is that if you've

67

got a bad slot machine, you will simply step over and play a new one.

Kmart, a major discount store chain, is also using subliminal techniques. Their management has known for a long time how to lower their lights just as readily as the casinos. They've also known how to captivate susceptible minds by flashing blue lights to announce specials. Kmart is also doing something fascinating with their mood-setting store music. We've known in industrial psychology that playing the right kind of music will increase worker performance and decrease worker tension. This successful discount chain has taken the music concept one step further. They're now combining hidden subliminal messages with the music they play during all store hours. Their money-saving message is, "Please don't steal!" Kmart found that their incidents of shoplifting went down by almost 30 percent within just a few months of using this tactic. They also found that sales increased substantially. Subliminal suggestion does work!

## POINTS TO PONDER

Have you ever been face-to-face with a new prospect or existing client who gave you the impression that you weren't getting through to him? Have you ever had a prospect who didn't quite see, hear, and feel the same level of motivation about buying your product as you do? Is your closing rate, or the rate at which people say yes to you when you ask for their business, less than 100 percent? Then read on..............

My company has done two years of research on the most productive, profit-making salespeople in America. Individuals were selected based on those who exceed one million dollars annually in commissions. We looked at people like Dennis Renter in Newport Beach, California; Murray Nielson in Vancouver, British Columbia; and Russ Gills in Virginia Beach, Virginia. They are all people who make enormous amounts of money in sales What are they doing? How do they make telephone calls? How do they write letters? Are they doing direct mail? How do they close? How do they present? We even asked them to tell us why, in their opinion, they were so successful. At the end of our two year study do you know what we found out? *They didn't know!!* But we discovered that by the time these enormously gifted high producers started making more than one million dollars in commissions, they had learned how to sell their prospects exactly the way their prospects wanted to buy. Those individuals we studied, who were making less than one million dollars a year, sold as though they were selling to themselves. The lower producers were not able to sell to those who were different from themselves. They were only able to close sales with people who possessed the same personality traits they did, people they could identify with easily.

## CUTTING-EDGE RESEARCH

Much new research in sales psychology has been done during the last decade. Use this information and you will discover how to determine, within thirty seconds of meeting a prospect, how he will decide to buy from you. 1) You will learn to observe, predict, and direct people. 2) You will understand how to observe people so well you'll be able to predict how they will buy in many situations. 3) You will be able to control yourself in dealing with them.

This research has led to quick and simple techniques for turning prospects into clients and doubters into customers.

A realtor in Wisconsin told a story about a self-employed prospect who was in need of a new investment property. While the property seemed to fit the prospect's financial goals, he procrastinated making a decision until the property was sold to another buyer. In frustration, the agent asked his prospect why it had taken so long to act. The prospect replied that the high price made him nervous. He said he didn't feel he understood the terms well enough to make a decision.

If the realtor could have communicated his suggestions more effectively and had read the prospect's initial uneasiness, would the prospect have been better served? It is enormously difficult to communicate meaning, let alone the intent of a message. This is due largely to the different experience levels of your clients and the different ways in which they process information into their minds. We metaphorically play a game of tennis with our clients when we communicate with them. We watch most of our ideas hit the net or go out of bounds. If you don't know your client's style of play, it's tough to keep the ball in the court.

People tend to think in three basic ways, as 1) *visuals,* 2) *auditories* or 3) *kinesthetics. Visuals* make sense of words by constructing or recalling images in their mind. If they can't make a picture from what you're saying, they may have trouble understanding your ideas. Auditories make decisions largely on the basis of how things sound. They often talk to themselves internally in order to comprehend a message.

*Kinesthetics,* on the other hand, tend to feel. They experience visceral gut-level emotions from talking to you. They may feel hot or cold about you after just a few minutes. If you knew what system your client was using to evaluate your ideas, would you be more effective? Of course you would!

Well, play a simple game with me. Think about your first hour of wakefulness this morning. What do you remember best? Think about what you saw, what you heard, and what you felt. What stands out most in your mind? If you remember more of what you saw, you are probably more visually based. If you remember more of what you heard, you are probably more auditory. If what you felt this morning sticks out in your mind, chances are you are *kinesthetically* based.

If a salesman could find out which one of these you are, *visual, auditory or kinesthetic,* would he be able to sell you more quickly? If you're a *visual,* and a salesman could quickly determine that you are a sight-based person, would he develop rapport with you more quickly? If he could get greater rapport, would he be able to get more trust? Well, I have great news for you. When people feel trust they buy. Without trust you could literally give money away and no one would take it. If I could show you a technique that in thirty seconds could help you determine whether your prospects are a *visual, auditory or kinesthetic,* would you be able to gain more rapport and thereby get more trust? If you could get more rapport and trust, would you then be able to increase your sales? There are two techniques that you will learn from this chapter on how to determine whether your prospect is a *visual, auditory or kinesthetic:* 1) By the way and direction they move their eyes when they think, and 2) by the words and predicates they use when talking, even on the telephone.

## VISUALS

*Visuals* possess minds that work like viewmasters. Do you remember playing with those little periscope-like toys that had circular slides when you were young? A lever advanced each picture, showing a three-dimensional view of the world. There were gorgeous scenes of places you weren't ever going to be able to visit. That's how *visuals'* minds work. They love looking at things they can see. They understand concepts that give them beautiful pictures. In fact, about 35 percent of your prospects fit into this category. They understand your ideas because of the images they have. They translate all your words into pictures they can comprehend, thereby gaining rapport and trust with you. They are the types of prospects who like bar charts, graphs, beautiful scenes, things that help them think readily in pictures.

Two athletes who knew how to use their sight-based talent to become winners are Dan Fouts and Billie Jean King. Dan Fouts is the quarterback for the San Diego Chargers.

Fouts has one of the best passing arms in all of pro football. One way that he has been able to play quarterback for so long is through his development of, "the timing pass." Before wide receiver Charlie Joiner retired, Fouts threw the ball to him in a pass play before Joiner turned around. As soon as Joiner turned, the ball hit him in the numbers. It was timed so precisely that the linebacker and other defenders couldn't intercept Fouts's passes. A linebacker usually waits for a receiver to turn around. This is his clue that his receiver will get the pass—one he can intercept. If the receiver turns at the last second, the linebacker hasn't got a chance. One day, a reporter asked Fouts how he did it. Fouts replied, "I go back in the pocket to pass. I look at a pass pattern in my mind. I see my receiver going down and out, fly pattern, curl around and then I see an X in the middle of my mental playing field where I'm about to throw the football. I throw the ball to the X in my mental map. If he's there, he catches it. If he's not there, nobody catches it." Fouts is a *visual*. He throws the football better than anyone else because of the *visual* image he makes of the pass patterns.

The great female tennis star, Billie Jean King was interviewed by Bud Collins, the *Boston Globe* reporter. He asked her how she kept such a high degree of concentration when hitting forehands and backhands on the court. Billie Jean said, "I can actually see the seams in the tennis ball as it travels across the net to me."

*Visuals* will give you certain cues to show you how they think. Watch their eyes. They move their eyes in three basic directions. You were probably told in your first sales training course, "Always watch your prospect's eyes." Did anyone explain why you should watch those eyes? Visuals will look up to the right when thinking about future information. When *visuals* construct and create, they look obliquely up to the right. You may ask a question such as, "Mr. Prospect, how much money do you expect to make this next year?" If that *visual* looks up to the right, he's constructing or creating a number. He may even be estimating and seeing a number inside his mind. If that *visual* looks up to the left, he's recalling

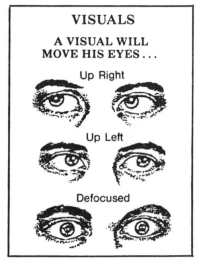

**VISUALS**

**A VISUAL WILL MOVE HIS EYES...**

Up Right

Up Left

Defocused

past information, things he's seen before. You may ask that prospect the question, "Have you ever bought a computer system?" If he looks up to the left, he's actually searching his memory for pictures of computers, trying to determine if he's ever looked at one for purchase. Finally, *visuals* may move their eyes into a defocused blank stare. Have you ever noticed, when some prospects are face-to-face with you, they stare right through you or give you a blank glazed look? When your prospect does this, he's actually synthesizing and translating your words into pictures he can understand more quickly.

Even the words these people use are *visually* based. If looking at eyes seems too difficult for you, Your prospect's words will prove to be a simple giveaway. *Visuals* use words such a *look,* ("that looks good to me"), or *clear,* ("that's clear so far"), or *see,* ("I see what you mean"), or *view,* ("here's my view on this *perspective",* or, "here's my perspective"). People don't use words randomly. When your prospect talks, he's giving you specific information about how he thinks. If he thinks in visual pictures, he will tell you by the use of his words exactly what's going through his mind. That's how people think and that's how they will buy.

Use specific strategies when dealing with *visuals.* 1) Draw pictures on paper when presenting ideas. 2) Talk with your hands. *Visuals* describe those who practice this technique as "charismatic." These ideas allow *visuals* to picture your message. 3) When showing a *visual* a fact sheet, hand it to him and stop talking. When your prospect is done processing the information, he'll re-establish eye contact. 4) Watch what you wear. Color research has shown that *visuals* may rate you higher in credibility when you wear blues and grays instead of browns or beiges, and of course, when you are well groomed.

The most important thing to do with *visuals* is to match their predicates and use their words. If you remember nothing else, please remember this. *Visuals* want to hear specific words from you that describe your product clearly. They want those words to be *visual* sight-based predicates. Phrases that help them access their natural thought picture system quickly are: "Do you *see* what I'm talking about? What's your *view* on this? In your *perspective*, does this seem as if it will work for you? So far, you've noticed the house has a gorgeous *view* from the veranda. How does this *look* to you? Do you *envision* this as the house you would like to spend the next few years in?" If you use *visual* sight-based words on your visual prospect, he'll buy from you more easily.

I have two kids, all boys except for one. My son, Neil, is twelve now; my daughter Stacey is four. There's a big age difference between them. When Stacey was born, Neil was very jealous of all the attention that she received from Mom and Dad. Neil became so resentful of the attention that he would find ways of getting back at Stacey, blaming his loss of parental attention on her. When Stacey was one year old, she walked on one foot at a time like a drunken sailor. In effect, she was off balance 50 percent of the time with each step. Neil would walk by Stacey and nudge her when she was on one foot. She'd fall down, then Neil would run away. I could never catch him doing this, although I could hear Stacey cry. One day I caught Neil red-handed. I said, "Neil, did you make Stacey cry? Did you knock her down?" Neil looked at me and said, "Dad, I was in the garage, playing. I heard her screaming and I came in to help." Of course he denied everything. I decided to give him his first psychology lesson. I said, "Neil, if you make Stacey cry, I make you cry." Nine years old at the time, Neil looked up at the ceiling and said, "Dad, I'm too old to get spanked." I discovered right away that Neil was making pictures by looking up at the ceiling. So I decided to use *visual* words to help him see what would happen to him the next time he hurt Stacey. I said, "Neil, look at me. Do you know what Stacey looks like when you knock her down? Tears run down her face. I grit my teeth when I see this happening. Then I clench my fists." I said, "Do you know what this means Neil?" Neil said, "You're ticked off, aren't you? I see what's going to happen to me the next time I do this. I'm sorry, it won't happen again." When I painted a picture for him, he certainly understood what would happen to him the next time he hurt Stacey.

I think my daughter, Stacey, is a *kinesthetic* and not a *visual.* Before I left on my latest trip, I walked up to her and said, "Stacey, sweetie, give me a kiss bye-bye." She turned away. Stacey has associated that when she kisses Daddy goodbye, Daddy leaves. Don't kiss Daddy, Daddy won't go. I held out my arms to Stacey and said, "Stacey, give me a kiss goodbye, please." She turned away again. I said, "Stacey, sweetheart, who loves Daddy?" She said, "Noooobody."

## AUDITORIES

*Auditories,* on the other hand, tend to think in a sound-oriented mode. They make sense of your message by recalling past conversations. They may also evaluate your ideas primarily on the sound of your voice and the delivery of your message. The world renowned tennis star, Jimmy Connors, plays "by ear." In the late 1970s, I had the opportunity to play against him in a professional tournament. Jimmy Connors beat me so badly that I walked off the court and sat on the sidelines with a towel over my head. In my case, it was not to blot up the sweat. I was hiding from embarrassment. Jimmy Connors, in those days, had the best return of serve on the pro tour.

He was the only guy who could return Roscoe Tanner's 138-m.p.h. serve, and actually hit winners off of it. This means he hit it back so hard that Tanner never got a chance to touch the ball. I decided to turn my horrible tennis defeat into a learning experience, so I approached him and asked, "Jimmy, how do you return serve so well? What do you think about? What goes through your mind? Do you lean forward on the balls of your feet? Do you block your shots back? Do you slice your back hand? Do you top spin your forehand?" Jimmy Connors replied, "I return serve better than anybody on earth because I listen to the way the ball sounds as it comes off the server's racquet." He said, "I can hear whether it will be a top spin, American twist, slice, or a flat serve. I can hear what the ball will do. When I know what kind of serve has been hit, I then simply anticipate, approach, and return." It's usually game, set, match, Connors. The man is an *auditory*. He returns well because he listens to how the ball is served.

*Auditories* also move their eyes in three distinct directions as they think to let you know that they are actually hearing sounds in their head. When *auditories* move their eyes directly side right, they are constructing and creating sounds in their heads. For example, you might say to a prospect, "What are your future needs for this product?" He may move his eyes to the right, thinking, "If I talk to my boss this afternoon, what will he say he wants?" They are in effect hearing future sounds. If they move their eyes to the left, they are hearing past sounds. For example, you may say to the prospect, "Have you ever heard of our company before?" If he moves his eyes to the left, he is searching his memory banks for the sound of the

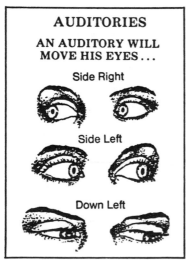

AUDITORIES

AN AUDITORY WILL
MOVE HIS EYES...

Side Right

Side Left

Down Left

company's name or motto. When a prospect looks down and to the left, he may be having internal dialogue. Down left eye movement indicates that your prospect is actually talking to himself, hearing his own conversation. *Auditories* also use key words to let you know they are thinking in sounds. They may use such words as *ring* ("that rings a bell"), or *sounds* ("It sounds good to me"), or *hear* ("I hear you"), or *say* ("I like what you're saying"). My mother used to say, "Don't take that tone with me young man." Obviously, listening to the words they use is even easier than watching their eye movements. Both, will give you a sure-fire tool to determine whether your prospect is actually thinking *auditorily.*

Here are some specific strategies to use with *auditories:* 1) Match their own predicates. Use phrases such as, "I'll bet that *rings* a bell" or, "Does that *sound* good to you?" Another phrase might be, "Do you like what you are *hearing?*" By using these *auditory* leading words, you'll help sound-based prospects understand your message much more quickly.

The real problem is not that you won't be able to sell without using the right strategies. The problem is that you won't sell as rapidly. If you are a *visual,* you probably sell to people *visually.* If you are a feeling-based *kinesthetic,* you tend to sell everyone else in the same feeling way. A good example of this was illustrated in the movie, *Ghost Busters.* One of the first scenes in the movie was in a library. Cards were spontaneously flying out of the catalogue card drawers. There was slime on the books and walls. Actor Bill Murray actually got slime on his hands and started wiping them across the books. Then Dan Akroyd, the great comedic actor, immediately said, "Listen, did you *smell* that?" Akroyd actually was mismatching predicates. You may also be mismatching your prospects. If you are a *visual,* you might say, "How does this look to you?" Your prospect may be an *auditory.* He would be thinking, "I really don't understand what you're talking about, I don't see pictures at all." The biggest reason why you're not closing more business could be that you are mismatching your prospect's buying mode. The people you want to close may not possess the same thought mode system as you.

Auditories frequently establish rapport more quickly with people who possess a disk-jockey-like resonance in their voices. They often have internal conversations with themselves, trying to make sense out of information. They may also have extended conversations or talk to themselves just to think. I knew a physician a few years ago who would literally talk himself through a decision--out loud! He would sit next to a staff nurse and ask her a question she couldn't possibly answer. He would then answer it himself and thank her for the help in solving the problem.

A financial salesperson in Florida, June Williams, found out how easy it is to sell to an *auditory* by using hearing-based techniques. She was trying to sell an insurance plan to a physician. About ten minutes into the presentation of showing pictures, drawings, illustrations, and giving *visual* examples, the prospect said, "Wait a second, June. Time out. Just talk to me about this. Explain it to me. Describe it to me. I don't want to look at all these charts, graphs, and brochures." June mistakenly said, "If I don't show you these charts and illustrations, you really won't understand the plan." He looked at her, smiled, and said, "Try me." June said okay, and did precisely that. She put all her felt pens and charts away and just talked with her prospect for a few minutes without the use of any *visual* aids. As she spoke, the physician leaned back in his chair, closed his eyes and started smiling. She thought he was fantasizing and said, "Listen! If you're going to ignore me, I'm going to walk out of here right now." In spite of her hostile remark the physician opened his eyes, winked at her, and said, "How much do I need to give you to get this plan started right now?" This man was an *auditory*. He didn't want to look at her charts, he wanted to listen. He was much more motivated by hearing the financial plan than he was by looking at it. Fortunately, he told June how he wanted to be sold. Most of your prospects will not tell you how they want to buy. They will just say, "No," without giving an explanation. If you don't sell to them in their unique thinking mode, they won't buy. If you can keep rapport high by matching their buying mode, you'll double your sales.

The second technique is to tickle their ears. My own financial planner in Orange County, California, unconsciously uses rhyme as he speaks. He presents insurance products to me by saying, "Kerry, keep your family protected. You don't want to die and leave them financially abjected, dejected or rejected." The third way to tune in to *auditories* is to select the correct background office music. Research done at Wal-Mart, a large discount store chain, found that when slow music was played, sales were substantially higher than when faster music was broadcasted. While *visuals* may not even notice the music is on, *auditories* will find their moods affected by it. A broker in Dallas uses a personal background stereo system in his office so he can control the type of music played. He plays classical music during probing, data gathering interviews, and faster paced melodies when he wants his *auditory* clients to make decisions and act quickly. The Musak Corporation has spent millions of dollars researching the types of tunes and tempos that will produce the highest levels of worker performance. They literally can prescribe Musak that speeds workers up after lunch or even slows them down toward quitting time.

The fourth technique is to explain illustrations as you proceed during a presentation. With *visuals,* you may find that they would rather read the illustration themselves while you remain quiet. *Auditories* prefer to have you explain it to them.


## KINESTHETICS

*Kinesthetics,* are feeling-based people. They feel hot or cold

79

about almost everything they experience. When these feeling-based individuals read a book or watch a movie, they may not

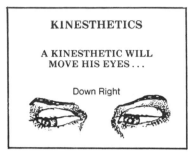

**KINESTHETICS**

**A KINESTHETIC WILL MOVE HIS EYES...**

Down Right

simply view it as entertainment, but they also experience it. Such people will reject or accept ideas on the merit of how they "felt" during exposure to them. Often athletes exhibit *kinesthetic* behavior. They, after all, gain great enjoyment from feeling or experiencing a sport. Many athletes say they love to play because it makes them feel good. Tennis star John McEnroe was once asked by television correspondent Bud Collins why he kicked a chair out from under an official line judge. McEnroe said, "I *felt* like it."

A prime example of an athlete who is a *kinesthetic* is Wayne Gretsky. This great Canadian hockey player has broken nearly every world hockey record. Wayne earns a salary of $800,000 a year as a player for the Edmonton Oilers. I asked Wayne about what goes through his mind before he makes those incredible goals. He said, "Kerry, most of the time I'm double or triple teamed. I can't even see the net. But you know, when I have that little black puck near my stick, I suddenly get a visceral feeling in my stomach that says, "Wayne, shoot the puck! If I shoot, it goes in! Or I will hit to my right wing, Jari Kurri, and he will shoot it in. It's usually point, hat trick, game, Gretsky!" The man is a *kinesthetic*. He feels the game. He's not like Fouts who makes pictures, or like Connors who hears sounds. He feels it, he makes the shot.

*Kinesthetics* will show you their thought processes by the way they move their eyes and the words they use. *Kinesthetics* typically move their eyes in only one direction: down to the right. This indicates they are thinking in a feeling-based mode.

You can also determine *kinesthetic's* thought processes

through specific words they tend to use. You will hear them use predicates such as, "It sure made an *impression* on me; How does that *grab* you; Let's *touch* base next week; Here's how I *feel* about it; It really *touched* me." Here are some tips to use with *kinesthetics*. 1) Match their words. Use phrases like, "What's your *feeling* on this? What's your *impression* of this? Shall we *touch* base next week?" If you use these predicates, they'll understand by getting a feeling for the meaning behind your message. 2) Give them things to touch. Since they are feeling-based, they are likely to develop an emotion around ideas you make tangible, so tangible they can literally touch it. Have you ever noticed that some prospects actually reach out and grab brochures as you talk? These *kinesthetic* prospects are showing you how to sell them more quickly.

Are you excellent at dealing with your prospect's resistance either over the telephone or face-to-face? If you are good, you probably know the feel, felt, found technique of overcoming objections. Here's how it works. If your prospect says it's too expensive, your response would be, "I understand how you feel. Others have felt the same way until they found the difference between price and cost. Price is what you spend today. Cost is what you pay over the long run." Now that is a great objection-handling technique for which of the three groups - *visual, kinesthetic or auditory?* If you answered feeling-based *kinesthetic*, you are absolutely right.

For example, the program chairman of a Savannah, Georgia, sales association took me to dinner before I spoke to his group. He asked me for a five-dollar bill to hold. As I watched, he ripped it up. He promptly said, "This is how much the I.R.S. is taking out of every dollar of profit your business earns." Nobody knows better than I how much money in taxes I pay. But, this very *kinesthetic* representation gave me a real feeling for how much I was losing. *Kinesthetics* desire to experience your ideas instead of just seeing or hearing them. When you present an idea to a *kinesthetic,* give him a sheet of paper outlining your ideas for him to hold. Then, explain the message he is already holding. You may wish to help him experience your ideas by asking him to underline key concepts or benefits.

At this point, you may think you operate in all three modes—*visual, auditory* and *kinesthetic,* and can't confine yourself to one group. The truth is, even though you can think in all three ways, you usually focus one one mode, and so do your prospects. It's important to discover your prospect's central mode. What's even more important is to observe how they think when you are with them. If a prospect moves from one mode to another, and you move with him, you will be able to maintain his trust. A good example of this is talking to a prospect about a product like life insurance. If you talk about a death benefit, your prospect may move from *visual* to feeling *kinesthetic.* But if you continue in a *visual* mode when he has switched, you will mismatch him. He will then lose rapport and trust in you. However, if you see him go into a *kinesthetic* mode and you follow, you will maintain rapport and sell him through high trust.

## SUCCESS IN SUBLIMINAL SELLING

In summary, your client is likely to fit into one of these three modes. Yogi Berra, manager of the New York Yankees, profoundly said, "You can observe a lot just by watching." Your clients will understand the true meaning of your message more effectively if you consciously use the right tools to communicate with them. *Visuals* want to see a message; *auditories* are more easily influenced by perceived sounds; *kinesthetics* understand ideas more quickly by feeling.

A stockbroker friend has an innovative way of effectively applying these concepts. He had encountered a fairly high barrier to getting new business. His procedure on the telephone had been to tell prospective clients about his products, then state who had referred him. Next, he would ask if they wanted to set up an appointment with him. His hit rate with this method was about 20 percent. The only change he made in this process was to use the appropriate *visual/auditory/ kinesthetic* predicates during these telephone referral calls. He discovered that the task became much easier. He claims his production has tripled because he now listens to how his clients think instead of just what they say. If you use these techniques, it may make a better communicator out of you. GREATER SALES SUCCESS is the bottom line.

We will elaborate on matching your prospect's thought mode (psychological sliding) in the next chapter.

# PART 7

# PSYCHOLOGICALLY SLIDING YOUR PROSPECT

Now that you're familiar with subliminal selling skills, you're ready to take your next step to increase productivity. But will these techniques always work?

Tom, a broker in Southern California, presented a mutual fund investment to his clients. Having already invested their money in real estate tax shelters, Tom's objective was to amass enough of his clients' money over the next few months to be able to buy into even bigger investments. Describing the benefits to his clients, Tom said, "If we can put $10,000 each month into this fund, you'll be able to invest in bigger deals and obviously get a better return." His client asked, "How much will this mutual fund's cost?" "Well, it's a back end fund, which means that the greater the amount of time you keep it in, the less costs are incurred." The client said, "I think I'll just keep my money in the money market fund at the bank. We're only talking five or six months and it's very liquid." Tom discussed the mutual funds benefits further, but ran into substantial road blocks. Logic seemed not to prevail. How should Tom have handled the situation?

Have you ever done a great job of answering objections only to be shot down by an uninformed prospect or client?

Have you applied the best techniques available on getting around negative clients, yet nothing seemed to work for you? Psychological sliding may work well. In the previous chapters you read about the concepts on how clients think. To recap, they basically think in three modes, as *visuals, auditories or kinesthetics (kinos)*.

In using the psychological sliding techniques, the objective is to match your prospect's thought mode as closely as possible. For example, you would show ideas to a *visual* on paper, using his own *visual* words. An *auditory* would rather have you describe your ideas using words like hear, sound, or tune. *Kinos* want to feel your concepts. They pay most attention to how your message affects them viscerally and less so by what they see and hear. They also want you to use feeling-based words.

However, even if you apply these techniques skillfully, your prospects may still object to your ideas. Often they get stuck thinking about their objections. When they are focused so deeply on the objections, they sometimes fail to recognize the real benefits. For example, I recently saw a fish and chips commercial on TV. The waitress tried to get the customer to taste a fish dinner. With each plea, the diner said, "I don't like fish. Fish tastes fishy. I don't even like the way it looks. I'll stick to hamburgers." The waitress unconsciously understood that the customer was stuck in his perception of how the fish tasted and appeared. The guy probably fixated his objection in his *visual* mode. She blindfolded the diner, went back to the kitchen, and returned with a hot, aromatic fish. She placed it under his nose to smell. While he smiled at the pleasant aroma, she cut a piece and placed it in his mouth. The commercial closed with the customer ordering a third helping of fish.

Would she have been as effective if she had reasoned with him that fish was really nutritious? Or by logically explaining how unique it had been prepared? Probably not. But she switched modes and led him to a different area of thought process *(visual, auditory, kinesthetic)* where he didn't have an objection. Do you think people are too smart for this kind of technique, or that once they give you an objection, you must overcome it with a bulldozer? Fortunately, there is an easier way to get your prospect to buy. A little thought mode sliding will give you a much better chance for success. You simply need to change your client's focus of attention.

When I was in the market for a BMW automobile, the salesman showed me several models. He focused on the most expensive model, a 735i. Usually a $38,000 car when new, he just happened to have a demo for $32,000 that was also the maximum I was willing to pay. While I liked the black exterior color, I hated the same black interior. When I told him this, he smiled and told me to sit in the driver's seat. He then requested that I close my eyes while he *kinesthetically* guided my feelings everywhere from how comfortable the seats were to how the gear shift knob felt in my hand. I have to admit, when he closed me, I went for that car, hook, line, and sinker. I bought because of my feeling. Unfortunately, for the car salesman, my wife, a *visual,* physically prevented me from signing the sales contract, much like a pet owner holding back a salivating dog from its dinner.

This salesman simply realized unconsciously that I had a major objection to the color. In fact, he sensed that I was vehemently opposed to black interiors. So he psychologically slid me from *visual,* where my objection was centered, to a *kinesthetic,* or feeling mode. He was a successful salesman because he was sharp enough to replace bulldozer objection fighting techniques with the more effective slide.

## THREE RULES

I recently studied a new psychological therapy where this technique was used to cure migraine headaches. Because of the excruciating pain, migraine sufferers are sometimes incapacitated for hours, and even days, at a time. One enterprising psychologist, realizing the limitations and harmful side effects of drugs, tried instead to refocus his patient's thought systems. Migraine sufferers are usually focused on pain, a *kinesthetic* experience. Through mild suggestion, the therapist urged sufferers to imagine the last time they had had an enjoyable experience without the migraine. He then asked them to visualize the details of the surroundings related to that enjoyable experience. He also requested that they recall what they heard during that experience as accurately as possible. He even went so far as to coax them into smelling the memories. The patients reported a much shorter duration of pain due to rerouting their focus of attention. The therapist psychologically slid the patients into experiences other than the *kinesthetic* ones where the pain of the migraine was concentrated.

The rules of psychological sliding are: 1) *Pace your client's though mode.* You will build rapport and trust much more quickly if you use the words and phrases' discussed in the previous chapter, that fit his natural thinking style. 2) *Try unobtrusive objection-handling techniques like,* "Why do you ask?" or, "Why is this important to you?" Your client may simply be requesting more information. If he still objects then go to rule 3. 3) *Go to an alternative thought mode.* For example, if your client says, "I don't feel this fits my business," then move him smoothly into *visual* or *auditory*. For example, "Tom, I know how you feel. I had a client a while back who felt the same way about this fund. I think you'll see after six months, that this will perform substantially better than any money market account. The picture I'm painting for you is that your return will be greater in the short run, even with commissions considered. Is your view consistent with this picture?"

A fairly seasoned broker was explaining the structure of a financial product to her client. After determining that he was *visual,* she drew pictures and charts, and produced company-published illustrations. During the stage when she ended her presentation, she sensed the client was losing interest. She asked him if there were any concerns. He told her he didn't think it fit his goals. She said, "Why do you mention this?" He told her he had seen some bad publicity on the company. The broker put her illustrations, charts, and graphs down, and psychologically slid into the *kinesthetic mode*. She told him a story about past clients in his age and income range who felt grateful to her that they had invested with the company. She moved closer, touched him on the arm, and expressed her feelings about the company's management leadership. With his focus of attention bridged from *visual* to *kinesthetic*, he became more thoughtful and contemplative. He appeared less preoccupied with his initial objection. Finally, he said to the broker, "Well, if you have this much faith in this company, I'll trust them too."

The next time you get a difficult objection, try psychological sliding. It will give you a very useful tool in increasing your closing rate to 100 percent.

Another essential technique, gaining trust from your clients, is discussed next.

# PART 8

# GAINING YOUR CLIENT'S TRUST

So far, you've learned many techniques on how your prospects and clients think. You've studied what makes them tick as well as how to read them like a book. This chapter, on developing trust quickly will stretch everything that you currently know about dealing with people. You will learn some advanced techniques dealing with people on a face to face basis, that will evoke rapport within just a few minutes. You'll learn what people really want from you, and how they treat their best friends. You'll learn which types of people they enjoy buying products and services from.

While reading this chapter, you'll learn that if you mirror and match your prospect's body language you can actually increase rapport. When you increase rapport, they'll increase their trust in you. You'll find out how to lead your prospects and clients to accept your ideas. Lastly, you'll learn how to match your voice to that of your prospect as you're speaking on the telephone.

## LOSING CONTROL

John, an experienced investment salesperson, was about to meet with a highly qualified prospect. Because of the strength of the referral, Bob (the prospect) agreed, without hesitation, to see John. Bob was an extremely successful business owner who had previously heard about John's services. After a solid handshake and introductory remarks, John sat in front of a large mahogany desk, while Bob leaned back in his high-backed, leather chair. Feeling a little anxious, John remembered his first course in sales training that taught salespeople to keep their cool and stay enthusiastic.

As Bob leaned further back in his reclining executive chair, John leaned forward toward, and soon onto, Bob's desk. While John realized that Bob was relaxed, he still wished Bob would show a little more interest and enthusiasm. John felt himself trying to speak faster. He moved closer still, and felt perspiration beading his forehead. He was losing control of the interview and the sale.

Have you ever found yourself in a situation like this? Have you ever wished you were able to generate rapport and trust with your prospect more quickly? Once you have gained your prospect's trust, he will buy almost anything from you as long as there is a need.

Trust is difficult to earn and rarely given quickly. Trust in business is defined as the belief in the competence of another person to complete the task at hand. If you believe that your prospect is able to help you achieve your goals in making a sale, and if he believes that you can give him the product or service he wants and needs, your sales cycle will shorten and your closing rate will go up.

To develop trust, you must first establish rapport with

your prospect. Rapport will not necessarily come from discussing football for a few introductory minutes. Although finding common social interests may be important, there is a quicker way.


## UNCONSCIOUS COMPETENCE

While doing research on client trust, I spent a few hours observing one of the best salesmen in recent memory, Dennis Renter. This million-dollar producing investment salesperson invited a couple to come into his office in Newport Beach, California. I played the part of a silent associate, sitting to the side and behind his prospects. Dennis immediately seated the couple at a small round table. He made sure that he sat within two feet of the man, who Dennis suspected was the decision maker. Dennis sensed some initial reluctance in his prospects. During his initial probing, Dennis spent about ninety seconds discussing the mutual friend who had referred the couple to him. After this brief exchange, Dennis questioned the prospects, asking for their short, medium, and long-term financial goals. I was astounded at how quickly this once-suspicious couple warmed up to Dennis.

Puzzled, I decided to stop listening to the verbal exchange and instead paid attention to what I was watching. What I observed surprised me. All three of them were in perfect synchrony. Every movement was duplicated by the other. Dennis' head tilted in exactly the same direction as both prospects. They leaned forward onto the table in identical fashion. Even their breathing rates were in unison. They were in such high rapport that I believe Dennis could have pulled out a photo of a used Chevy and made a sale.

I paid close attention to his next client as well. The same initial social amenities were exchanged. This time I looked for only non-verbal characteristics. The new prospect, a mid-level manager, was obviously as relaxed as Dennis. I noticed the prospect lean forward onto the conference table. Within a few seconds, Dennis also moved forward in his chair toward the table. What astounded me was how receptive the prospect became to Dennis shortly after these episodes. Later, I discussed what I had observed with Dennis. He was not aware of his non-verbal behavior. After twenty years of selling, he had become an "unconscious competent"—he was quickly able to generate trust, but he didn't know how he achieved that state.

Dennis's tactics run counter to generally accepted selling theories. You probably learned in sales training 101 that you must be enthusiastic and full of brisk energy. If you are energetic, your prospect will also become energetic. Nothing could be further from the truth. By watching miles of videotaped sales interviews, we have learned that even very articulate and product-aware salespeople often fail to close effectively because they haven't established a sufficient level of rapport and trust with their prospects during initial interviews.

## MIRROR YOUR PROSPECT

Frank Triolo, a top-producing salesman in Appleton, Wisconsin, closes nearly 100 percent of his prospects. He "mirrors" every nuance in his prospect's posture. When he goes into a prospect's or client's office, Frank waits to determine how the prospect will sit and immediately duplicates that posture. If Frank's prospect crosses his legs, Frank does the same. If the person leans forward, Frank follows suit. His mirroring behavior makes a lot of sense. Next time you're at a restaurant, try to spot a pair of lovers. They will invariably mirror each other's every gesture. They'll probably sit one to two feet from one another and engage in a kind of courtship dance. If one smiles, the other will smile. If one folds his arms, the other will unconsciously fold arms in exactly the same way.

Your first response may be that this behavior seems manipulative. Yes, it can be, if poorly done. However, the big hitters I have observed do it so elegantly, it becomes a normal part of the interview process. They usually first match the prospect's initial body posture. When the prospect moves to a new position, the peak producers will wait five to ten seconds, then slowly move to mirror the propect's new position. What could be more natural and comfortable in establishing rapport.

## LEADING YOUR PROSPECT

One of the most difficult tasks in sales is converting the apathy of a prospect into enthusiasm. Million-dollar producers have an uncanny way of using this rapport mirroring technique for that purpose.

Dennis Renter also uses a technique called "leading" to make his prospects more receptive. He matches and mirrors his prospect's body language until he feels rapport has been established. Then, he leads his prospect into increased interest by moving forward, causing the prospect to follow in the same manner. For example, have you ever seen Air Force jets flying in tight formation? The pilots usually try to line up the aircraft's nosc with the wingtip of the leading plane. After a few minutes in flight, these pilots report such a high level of flying rapport that they cease to be concerned about the forward wingtip. The planes in formation move as one single welded piece of flying steel.

One evening, I decided to test this mirroring and leading theory myself. I attended a reception the night before a conference at which I was to speak. The program chairman of the group held a drink in his left hand, and placed his right hand in his pants pocket. I likewise held a drink, but was motioning with my other hand. I noticed our mismatch in body posture. Our rapport level didn't seem as high as it could have been. I began to mirror my host. I put my drink in my left hand and my right hand into my pants pocket. I felt our rapport level rise. He became much more conversant and willing to speak candidly. Then, I decided to test our rapport level by trying to lead him. I removed my right hand from my pocket. Within five seconds, he also removed his right hand. Questioning him later, I discovered he was unaware of the technique I had used with him.

If you want to gain rapport quickly, mirror your prospect. But, if you want to lead them to your point of view, change your physical body language. If they do not in turn mirror you, your level of rapport is not high enough to move on toward the close.

At this point go back to mirroring your prospect again. Continue to match his body language until you feel rapport is high, then try leading your prospect again. It will work. It is very rare that two people in high rapport are not able to lead each other. By using these techniques, you'll be able to lead your prospect to exactly your own non-verbal body position.

## STUPID LIKE A FOX

The reason why this is so effective is because you can actually lead your prospects to espouse certain ideas or even change their attitudes just by virtue of the non-verbal body position in which you guide them. John Milam, a salesperson from Knoxville, Tennessee, had an appointment scheduled with a prospect. He arrived at the appointed time fully prepared to make a sale. Unfortunately, the prospect was nearly 30 minutes late. The prospect walked into the office, sat down and said, "John, I can't see you right now, I'm too busy." John saw that his prospect's arms were crossed. John in turn crossed his own arms and said, "When would you like to re-schedule this meeting?" They were obviously in a bit more rapport than when they first started. The prospect looked at John and said, "How long would this take if I were to see you right now?" John said, "10 minutes, unless you ask me any questions." They both walked back to the prospect's office where the prospect sat behind a desk in a high, wing-back chair, and proceded to cross his legs and arms. Obviously, this is a defensive posture.

Now guess what John did? If you thought that John mirrored the prospect, you're absolutely right. He casually crossed his legs and arms in the same fashion as his prospect. After four or five minutes, John realized that the prospect was getting more defensive. The prospect actually crossed his legs tighter, leaned further back in his chair, and then proceded to interlock his fingers behind his head. Have you ever seen a prospect do this before?

## THE PIECE DE RESISTANCE

Most successful and experienced salespeople realize that when a prospect leans all the way back in his chair, he is basically saying, "I don't respect you. I'm giving you a bit of my time, but there's nothing useful for me here." Guess what John did this time? You guessed it! John leaned back in his chair, crossed his legs, and in turn, interlocked his fingers behind his head. John wrote me a letter and said, "Kerry, we looked like a couple of plucked chickens." Then John did something that may have seemed stupid, but was actually quite brilliant. Immediately at the point he felt they were in the highest level of emotional rapport, he *leaned forward* in his chair. Then he moved slowly onto his prospect's desk. This is stupid if you remember hearing in basic sales training never to lean onto a prospect's desk when you're in his office. It's stupid unless the prospect does what? That's right! The prospect leans onto his own desk. This is fondly called a buying signal.

In the chapter on buying signals, two positions you will read about are the sitting tremor and whistling tea pot. Both describe your prospect leaning forward in his chair, thus indicating readiness to buy your product. This is your cue to stop talking and let him buy! John saw that his prospect had responded by leaning forward onto his own desk. This super salesman remarked, "We've said enough about this, haven't we?" The prospect replied, "Yes, we have." John said, "This investment will close out next week unless we take advantage of it right now. Let's do it." The prospect winked his eye and said "Great, why not?"

## NATURAL RAPPORT

In this case, John made a sale and turned around a negative prospect who, at first, wasn't going to see John at all. He turned an unimpressed prospect into one who was not only impressed, but who later bought. To say "no" to John, this prospect would have had to say "no" to himself, because John was able to mirror and match his prospect.

When people establish high rapport, they mirror and match each other naturally. Notice that when you move, people who feel close to you typically follow you. When one moves out of rapport, others will follow to re-establish that rapport. You've undoubtedly experienced this in a political conversation with someone. Did you also notice during your conversation, that you were in such high rapport that when that person made a comment, in opposition to your own, you were likely to accept it in an effort to maintain rapport with him. You would accept his ideas rather than cause dissonance by disagreeing with him. The same thing is true in non-verbal cues as well as with attitudes. Your prospect will struggle to create rapport with you in the first place and then will develop and maintain that rapport with you.

## MIRROR VOICE TEMPO AND TONE

In the preceding paragraphs, you learned that we tend to

trust others when we have rapport with them. Rapport exists in body posture, as well as in voice qualities. You probably are aware of the difficulties inherent in a New York City salesman trying to generate rapport with an Alabama prospect. The fast-clipped harshness of the New Yorker's voice would probably fail to generate trust from the slower-talking "down home" prospect. But are you also aware of some of the more subtle voice chararcteristics?

Peak performing salespeople like Craig Beachnaw, of Centennial Insurance in Lansing, Michigan, can do wonders on the telephone. Craig is able to raise or lower his voice pitch depending on his client's vocal qualities. He instinctively knows that if he talks in a deep bass tone, the prospect will lose rapport and trust unless the prospect's voice has the same characteristics. Most importantly, Craig has the ability to speed up his voice pace or slow it down. He fluctuated his voice speed depending simply on the way his prospects say hello.

Another voice expert is an executive who received an insurance settlement after he learned about these techniques. After his car was stolen, the executive spent weeks negotiating with his insurance company, both in person and on the telephone. He called the Des Moines headquarters from his office in Newark. He immediately became aware of the slower voice tempo and tone of the person on the other end. This pro changed his voice to match that of his listener. He reportedly not only received a larger cash settlement than expected, but the check was mailed the next day.

## CONCLUSION

If you have all the trust you want from your prospect, there is no need to use these techniques. You both will mirror and match each other without being consciously aware of it. But, if you constantly deal with new people who you must get to know quickly, you may wish to develop these techniques. Your closing rate is not as dependent on the product's technical features as it is on your prospect's trust in you. The top salesperson at an east coast company said at a recent conference that he doesn't sell products, he sells himself. The prospect then follows the buying recommendations based on his trust of the salesperson. This is a pretty impressive statement coming from a $1.3+ million producer. Your company is far more likely to saturate you with product details than ideas educating you in people skills. They seem convinced that their mousetrap is the best. They've missed the point of selling. *Your prospects don't buy products, they buy trust.* They often buy whatever you *recommend* because of that trust. Your prospects won't buy until they trust YOU! Prospects don't trust products, they trust people.

Once trust is established, determining your prospect's buying strategy is essential to making your sale. We shall discuss this strategy in the following chapter.

# PART 9

## DISCOVERING YOUR PROSPECT'S BUYING STRATEGY

Have you ever done a great job of solving your prospect's problems only to find that he eventually bought from someone else? In frustration, you found that you really wasted a lot of valuable time. Have you ever had a prospect who told you exactly what he needed and then changed his mind?

Remember the old adage, "Find a need and fill it?" Even if you do a great job of probing and presenting, you still may not be able to close 100 percent of the time. This is basically because even though you determined your prospect's needs (and got agreement), he still may not buy if you don't find out his *buying strategy*. Forget, for the moment, your ability to overcome objections and your favorite five closing phrases. Your prospect is more likely to buy from you if you first know how he has made buying decisions in the past.

Mike, an extremely successful insurance salesperson in Southern California, thought he had an airtight disability insurance sale. His prospect, Tom, realized that as a self-employed professional he needed financial protection from illness or accident. Mike determined Tom's average monthly income level, how long he could survive on savings alone and then prescribed the amount of monthly disability benefit. He got agreement from Tom on the product benefits and then closed him. Mike did an effective job of selling, right? Wrong. Tom procrastinated for a week and then bought from Mike's competitor. Why? Because Mike didn't determine Tom's psychological buying strategy, or how he made previous purchasing decisions.

Do you always know how your prospect will decide to buy? When you're booking an appointment from a telephone conversation, do you find out quickly how he will decide to give you an appointment, or when you do see him face-to-face, how he will decide to buy your product?

Once you learn to ask the right questions, you can acquire this information quickly. If you don't find out, ahead of time, *HOW* that prospect will buy or *WHAT* his decision-making strategy is, you'll never reach a 100 percent closing rate. But, if you do ask the right questions, your prospects will let you know, in advance, how they will buy. Learning this will help you know exactly what part of the product interests him the most, precipitating your prospect's decision to purchase.

## SUPPORT YOUR COMPETITION

Let's take a few different situations. Does your prospect already have a vendor? If you're a carpet salesman, does he already have a carpet? Will you have to compete against somebody else he's currently using? One rule of thumb is never to criticize competitors. There is a good reason to follow this code of conduct. Not only is it basically unacceptable to down-grade other professionals, but chances are, if you do criticize your competition, your prospect will defend that vendor, whether or not he likes the salesperson or their services.

Realizing this, you can discover a great deal about your prospect's relationship with the vendor by using phrases such as, "You use GPS Business Services? I've heard they are a good company. What do you like most about GPS?" Your prospect will reply, "The counselor is truthful. He's a good negotiator and he works very hard for me." Then you can say, "Sounds like you're very pleased with him." You're actually building him up to the point that prospect may, on the spot, tell you what he doesn't like about the vendor.

For example, I was in the midst of trying to secure a consulting contract with a large construction firm. When I telephoned my prospect from a referral lead, I asked some probing questions in an effort to find out his relationship with one of my competitors who was already being utilized by the company. He said, "We're already using Dan Thompson for sales training," I said, "Tony, I heard great things about Dan Thompson. What do you like about him?" "Well he's got good delivery. My salespeople seem to like him. He's on target with what they do, day in and day out."

I then said, "Sounds like he's doing a super job for you." At that point, my prospect backed down a little bit and started to be candid. I was, in effect building my competition up too much in my prospect's eyes, so that the prospect found a few faults. The prospect said, "Dan is good, but I would like to see more variety in his approach. He does basically the same closing program over and over again, and I don't think my salespeople find his sales techniques challenging." AH! A chink in the armor. I found out what my prospect disliked about my competition without making any disparaging remarks.

Of course, when talking about competition, you can use such phrases as, "Are you getting the satisfaction you want from your present vendor?" This may work, but be careful; your prospect may see this as a criticism, and defend the competition.

## DEFINE PERFECTION

Another great line is to ask your prospect is directly what, in his opinion, is "perfection." This is extremely effective in making introductory phone calls and probing for information. You might say something like, "Let's assume you really had perfection when working with a financial planner. What does a perfect financial planner mean to you?" This is an effective and informative question. The prospect undoubtedly has a clear idea of what he wants in a planner. Possibly your competition does not know this.

The answer your prospect may give is, "My idea of the perfect financial planner is someone I can trust to give me sound advice on my investments." This gives you a lot of information on what your prospect wants. He doesn't want specific products, he wants sound investment advice.

Your next question might be, "Are you getting that, right now, from your financial planner?" You see, you really can find out how people will buy if you ask them very simple questions.

## DISCOVER BUYING BEHAVIOR

Do you believe that people really can change any time they want to if there is enough need and motivation and a deep desire to effect that change? If you answered, "No, people really don't substantially change," you're absolutely right. However, they can go through dramatic behavior modifications. Here's a common example. Have you ever tried to quit smoking? You're probably saying, "Yes, of course, but I've never succeeded. I've tried to stop seventeen times." Behavior modification will allow you to quit smoking permanently, although it may take several attempts on your part. In the context of all the behaviors that make up who you are, smoking is a very small one. There's a lot more to you than that. But changing your smoking habit is an extremely difficult thing to do.

Recently, I bought two new tennis racquets. When I played on the pro tour in the mid-1970s, I used only composite-style wood racquets. They gave me more ball control. Even now, ten years after I played in the pros, I'm still buying the same kind of wooden racquets. Jimmy Connors, the fourth best tennis player in the world, is still playing with an outdated Wilson T-2000 racquet. Why? In the midst of space age racquets with bigger hitting zones, more power and greater control, why is he playing with a relatively antiquated racquet that plays like a trampoline? Because his playing and racquet-buying behaviors haven't changed (by the way he gets all the free racquets he wants).

## OLD SOLDIERS NEVER DIE

If your prospect has ever purchased a product in the past, even remotely similar to yours, he will use basically the same buying strategy in purchasing again. You can determine your prospect's strategic buying criteria simply by asking one or two questions. "How did you decide to buy the product before?" or "Why did you decide to buy that product before?" You will probably get answers like, "I bought it because the agent said it provides protection. He said the cash buildup would earn interest rates above what banks would pay." Regardless of what his needs are, this simple analysis determines that the prospect will probably decide to buy your product because it gives protection and pays interest on cash buildup above what banks would pay. Of course, you should fill his needs, but if you want to close that sale, you'll sell based on your knowledge of how he bought in the past.

Another question you might ask for more information is, "What would you like to improve?" The answer will provide you with further information on areas where he may be dissatisfied. Basically, this information will take you only minutes to obtain, but will literally put money in your pocket. Once you determine your prospect's buying strategy, you then simply use a concept called "instant replay." During the presentation stage of the interview, you "play back" or "replay" the same criteria your prospect just gave you in making buying decisions. You might say, "Mr. Prospect, I think you'll find that this product will offer you the protection we talked about, and will also pay you interest on the premiums. In fact, the interest rates are higher, after taxes, than what your bank is paying on your savings account."

If you learn your prospect's buying strategy, and play it back to him, you're going to close more business. To decide against buying from you, he would have to deny himself.

## THE HAPPY ENDING

After Mike had determined another prospect's needs on a life policy, he then asked, "Have you ever bought a policy before?" His prospect said, "Yes, I bought a term insurance policy a few years ago that has a face value of $500,000." Mike said, "Why did you buy it?" The prospect said, "I was in an airline accident a few years ago. My wife went crazy. She immediately called an agent for life insurance. But, I wanted to earn better interest rates on my money, so I bought low-cost term and put the money I saved in premiums into a limited partnership." "Is there anything you'd like to improve on the policy?" "Yes, but the agent has never once called to find out if everything was okay. I haven't seen or heard from him in three years."

Guess what Mike did? He jotted down these answers in his notes and then did an "instant replay" during the presentation stage. Mike simply said, "This universal life policy gives you the same benefits as your term insurance, and, in addition, gives you very high after-tax interest revenue. I promise you, I'll review your financial position yearly to make sure you have the right coverage for your income level." Do you think Mike got the business? You bet!

## FUTURE PLANNING

Have your ever had a prospect who has never bought a product like yours? Simply help this prospect project into the future. Use a phrase such as, "Mr Jones, you seem interested in purchasing life insurance. I want you to imagine, for a moment, that you've had our insurance policy for a year. During that year, how did you know that it was the best insurance investment for you?"

Listen carefully to his response. Suppose it goes something like this, "My family's future is well protected. . . . I'm building cash value. . . . the company that I purchased the policy from is a good, solid one." Guess how he will decide to buy insurance?

If you're sharp, you'll give him assurances that his family's future will not only be secure but, in addition, his new policy will be building cash accumulation value from a company that is highly rated within the insurance industry. When you meet with him, you will show him an illustration of his coverage and cash accumulation as well as a brochure about the insuring company.

## "AS IF"

Another psychological concept in probing or interviewing is

called the "as if" technique. Do you find that it is easier to sell to prospects who already know what they want? Do you ever interview prospects who don't already know what they want? The "as if" technique might help. But be careful. It may work so well, you could become a little lazy and spoiled.

You probably already know what he wants, but hasn't yet experienced it. Help him to experience your product before he buys it. Ask him this. "Mr Prospect, let's assume it is two years in the future. What happened during that period that let you know this was a good buy for you?" He might say, "Well, I was able to afford the payments and you saw me once each year to find out how my family was doing." Guess how you'll sell this prospect? You will literally prove to him that with current increases in earning power, he will be able to afford the payments. You will also need to prove that you'll see him once a year and won't leave him feeling like an orphan customer.

Another way you can work the "as if" technique is to ask him how you should sell him. You can do this simply by going into the near future and becoming a Monday morning quarterback. For example, in selling a prospect a limited partnership recently, a broker in California said, "Let's assume our talk is over. What happened that let you know this was a good investment for you?" His prospect said, "Well, I guess you were able to prove to me that the general partner knew what he was doing. You showed me that he could fulfill his promises. Also, the market was shown to be good for this kind of investment." The broker then simply incorporated these "concerns" into his presentations.

You see, by using the "as if" technique, you are literally bypassing the objection phase of the sale. By getting your prospect's strategies and concerns in advance, you are merely presenting useful and effective information in the way your prospect wants to hear it. Teach these techniques to at least two people in the next week. You will discover your own way to to apply these ideas, and will also remember them longer.

## ONE HUNDRED PERCENT

If a 100 percent closing rate is your goal, use these techniques. Your buyer's decision strategy is not as enigmatic as it seems. In fact, when you use these techniques, your prospect will create the sale and close himself for you. You'll end up with a satisfied customer and your highest production ever!

In the next chapter we'll discuss the fascinating effect color has on selling.

# PART 10

## INFLUENCING SALES WITH COLOR

Jill, a financial salesperson, was in the midst of presenting a product to her prospect. A smart dresser, she was well aware of appropriate business attire and style. During her presentation, the prospect 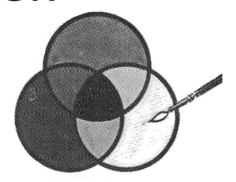 seemed uneasy. He fidgeted and seemed to have trouble listening to her. The prospect didn't buy. In fact, he didn't even come close. Little did Jill know that her black suit may have had a depressing effect on her prospect. The unconscious associations made by the prospect were black = death = dying = bad investment = treachery. Does this seem far-fetched to you? Consider that London's suicide bridge was named Black Friar's bridge. When the black bridge was painted a green hue, suicides dropped by over 33 percent.

Do you think color has an affect on you and your prospect's behavior? If you answered, "Yes," you are absolutely right. The newest research indicates that your prospect may buy more quickly, or not buy at all, just because of the influence of color. Does it seem to you that red cars go faster than brown ones? I recently spoke to a convention of Porsche dealers in Canada. They told me their most frequent color request was red. More red Porsches were sold than any other car color. Here's another question. If you were selecting a truck based on durability, reliability and power, would you choose yellow or black? General Motors Corporation reports that their top-selling pick-up truck colors are black and dark brown.

The effect of color persuadability has long been a focal point of sophisticated research. In the late 1970s, researchers from the University of California at Berkeley conducted a study within the California prison system. Prison guards were selected for participation in this project on the basis of strength and endurance. These guards were instructed to exercise with dumbbell weights. The subjects did as many repetitions of curls as they could.

One guard did an amazing twenty-eight curls without stopping. The same guard was then directed to curl the dumbbells again, as many times as possible, standing in front of one cubic foot of blue poster board. Even though fatigue had set in, he was still able to better his initial score by one, doing a total of twenty-nine curls while looking at the color blue.

For the final test, the same guard was again asked to curl the dumb-bells. This last time, pink was put in front of him, so that the only view he had was of the pink poster board. Guess how many he did with the color pink? He went from 28 curls with no color focus, to 29 curls looking at blue, down to 5 curls looking at pink. Strength, in this case, was definitely depreciated by viewing the color pink during the exercises. Unlike blue, pink has a weakening effect on physical strength. It causes the release of norepinephrine in the body, a chemical that inhibits activity of specific hormones which contribute to aggressive behavior. In fact, Hayden Frye, coach of the University of Iowa Hawkeyes football team, hasn't lost a home game in over seven years. His home locker room is painted blue. The visiting locker room is decorated in pink. The California prison system is now installing pink cells called "sedation cells" for unruly prisoners. When a prisoner becomes overly aggressive, the guards move him to a pink cell for about thirty minutes. The results have shown a decrease in aggressiveness, hostility, and violence in these inmates.

## THE COLOR OF MONEY

Typically the more money your prospects make, the more they are attracted to muted colors. The less money they make, the more they like brighter colors. Studies indicate there are three particular colors you can use with prospects who make over $40,000 a year. These three colors test best for comfort and persuadability with your affluent prospects. The first color is blue. It is the most formal color in the spectrum. It is also the favorite color of both males and females in America. In fact, it is highly atttractive to those individuals making very large purchases. It is also the IBM Corporation's nickname, "Big Blue." This top company did years of research to determine which color would have the greatest impact on those spending hundreds of thousands of dollars on computer systems.

The next color is dove gray. It is quickly associated with high socio-economic status. In fact, it is also a symbol of intelligence and quick decision making. It is the color most likely to attract upper income people. In fact, the Sharper Image Corporation, the company that will let you buy a yuppie toothbrush for $500, uses this color extensively. I was in Honolulu recently and noticed that their store was decorated in this color from floor to ceiling. When I asked the store manager if the color helped sell merchandise, she said that in the month since they had changed to the gray decor, sales increased by 25 percent.

The third best color is hunter green. It is the most soothing color to human beings. We associate it with currency, revenue, income, and profits. Color can work in two ways to influence you—psychologically and physiologically. Green influences you both ways.

## CULTURAL INFLUENCES

Much of our response to color is governed by our age and

gender. It is also affected by our socio-economic status, religion, climate, and racial background. For example, certain groups of your prospects may be influenced by dramatically varied colors. Low economic or lower middle-class prospects may respond best to colors in their purest form. They may enjoy strong reds, hot oranges, bright blues, and vivid greens. They may not appreciate delicate tones as readily as higher socio-economic status prospects. Some social researchers have conjectured that people in the lower classes of society may live in relatively drab, blighted surroundings. The vivid colors they find attractive probably add vibrancy to their lives. Middle class prospects may enjoy a broader range of colors. They are attracted to color blends created by mixtures such as a bright red with brown to form a shade of maroon.

## TRIGGER COLORS

I am often asked about a color that seems to draw attention everywhere—vivid red. In research with racing horses, stables were painted red-orange or blue. In the blue sections, the horses quieted down much more rapidly. In the red-orange sections, horses remained hot and restless. Consequently, many more flies were found in these red stables. In experiments on monitoring heart rate, red was shown to have an accelerating effect. Blue and green slowed vital signs. While red is a useful attention-getter, it may spell danger, stop, warning, blood, murder and violence. It may be wise to underline an idea on paper in red to gain attention, but counter productive to color an ad or brochure in red. It's okay to use red lettering or wear a red tie, but never red brochures or red packaging unless you're wrapping up a Porsche.

Just as there are three "positive" colors, there are also three "negative" ones. The worst of these colors is black. Although it is currently a fashionable color for women's clothes, culturally it is closely attuned to mortality. This dark color is often associated with nightmares and impending doom. Don't ever wear this color when you sell. Journalist Nicholas Daniloff was psychologically tortured by the KGB during his two-week interrogation at Moscow's Lefortovo prison. His cell was painted black to induce depression, making the reporter more malleable to his KGB interrogators. This color will depress you within forty-five seconds. Avoid black in brochures, handouts at meetings, and especially in your suit. You may look like a funeral director wearing black.

The second worst color is purple. It is best to limit the use of this color; it is one that gives mixed messages. Dramatic and diverse interpretations are associated with purple. On the one hand, it has historically denoted royalty and grandeur in Western Europeran cultures. Both kings and queens wore it. However, this color is also often associated with sickness and vomiting. It is interculturally linked to illness.

When a Japanese Kabuki dancer wears a headband with this color, the audience knows the character is extremely sick. In the United States, military services award a medal in this color to any military person wounded in active combat. If you are Catholic, you know that this color is draped over the cross during Lent as a sign of mourning.

The third worst color, yellow, seems to stimulate anxiety more than any other. It is the most irritating color to the retina in the eye of those over fifty years of age according to color researcher, Faber Birren. It is also a color which can increase blood pressure within thirty seconds. This color is the recommended necktie shade by the *Wall Street Journal* this year. Interestingly, both males and females seem to dislike yellow-green intensely. You probably use a yellow pad in front of your prospects when taking notes. Since it may adversely affect them, why not use a green pad or even a blue or gray note pad. Judging from the length of time your prospect spends looking at your note pad, it could influence his buying behavior.

Do you use transparencies or flip charts in your presentation? An associate of mine, Linda Woods, a California color researcher, suggests that white on overheads or flip charts causes a kind of snow blindness. Extra light constricts the eye pupil, which also fatigues the ocular muscles. Instead, you might consider using green transparencies or even a colored flip chart.

Horticulturists have long known that certain types of colored fluorescent lights will increase a plant's growth rate. Research on rats has led biologists to determine that the color of the environment can influence the sex of rat offspring. It is also logical to surmise that color can have a psychological and physiological effect on human beings.

## APPETIZING HUES

Color can even influence your appetite. It may help you lose weight. Would you like to hear about this? You're probably thinking, Kerry I've got furniture disease, my chest has fallen into my drawers. A rainbow color that may increase your appetite is frequently utilized by expensive restaurants to discourage guests from taking fifty-dollar-a-plate meals home in doggie bags. They decorate their table cloths and napkins in red in an effort to get you to eat more. This color also will increase your metabolism rate. If you are on a diet, don't let anyone put red in front of you.

The color most likely to decrease appetite is one utilized by unsuspecting greasy spoon restaurants, it is blue. Unaware that they're depressing patrons appetites, these establishments are often painted in the owner's favorite color.

The Holsum Bread Company found that it's sales soared when they changed wrappers to red-orange, an "edible" color. Conversely, biologists report humans have a natural aversion to blue-tinted foods. We won't eat blue food. Have you noticed even blue decorations on the table may affect our appetite. A nutritionist friend of mine determined that those who need to diet should eat meals while looking at blue. She also has a sure-fire technique to determine if you are overweight. All you have to do is stand in front of a full-length mirror, take all your clothes off, jump straight up and straight down, then look at your watch. If you feel body movement after four minutes, you're overweight.

## COLOR RESEARCH

Color research is a rapidly developing field. Unfortunately, most experimentation is conducted in Europe and Russia. In the United States, we are lagging behind in our understanding of how color affects our emotions. We are just now starting to learn such things as what colors will help people buy more quickly. Corporate revenues depend on our understanding of people. If you evaluate your marketplace and select appropriate colors that are most appealing to your prospects, you'll have an influential edge over your uninformed competitors.

Like color, one's personal attire can affect production. We'll discuss your image in the next chapter.

# PART II

# USING IMAGE TO INCREASE PRODUCTION

Image experts have told us time and time again that expensive, well-fitting suits command respect. They have also told us that cheap and/or poorly selected, bad-fitting suits can contribute to lost business. But have you paid much attention to the ties you wear? They too, may factor into the level of acceptance you receive from both clients and prospects. If your clients feel great acceptance of you, you will gain higher rapport with them. When you have higher rapport, you'll get higher trust. When you have trust, you get business.

## HISTORY OF THE TIE

During the Renaissance, ties were worn only by the wealthy for a very special purpose. Ties served as a bib for the wearer during meals. The aristocrat would also use his tie as a napkin after eating. In our day, males often toss their ties over their shoulders when they eat to prevent the tie from getting food on them. The shape of the tie has evolved from a very wide piece of fabric to a very narrow piece of clothing used as an accessory.

# HOW TO WEAR TIES

It is important to know how to wear a tie. A tie should extend down to at least the belt. In fact in some areas of the U.S., it is very fashionable to wear it two or three inches below the belt. It should be securely fastened at the neck in a full Windsor knot. An easy way to determine a "Sunday-only tie wearer" is when his tie extends only to the top of his pot belly.

Just as important is the fabric from which the tie is made. The most accepted material today is silk. Most polyester/silk blends look like blends. By all means avoid polyester ties no matter what volume discount you received. If you can tell the difference between a polyester and a silk tie, so can your clients.

# TYPES OF TIES

The five most popular types of ties are: 1) the Rep or diagonally striped tie, 2) the foulard tie, 3) the club tie, 4) the polka dot tie, 5) the solid tie. Bow ties, except when worn with tuxedos, are rarely seen in fashionable circles.

## The Rep

The most universally accepted and useful tie is the Rep. Once identifying the military rank of the wearer, it must always be clear edged (the colors must be separate, rather then blending together). It is widely accepted because it can be worn while doing business with blue collar workers and business managers alike. It has less snob appeal than other ties and will gain acceptance from a wide variety of clients.

## The Foulard

The foulard tie (traditionally small circles or triangles on a woven silk background) is the Ivy League look of the 1980s.

This tie is seen atop Brooks Brothers' shirts of the very rich. It suggests an image of, "I went to Harvard." As you might have guessed, the foulard style originated in the conservative Northeast, where only the most wealthy wore them. In fact, Ronald Reagan almost exclusively wears foulards. If you have an appointment with a CEO, an owner of a fairly large company, or a highly affluent professional, you may make extra points by wearing a foulard.

I once spoke to a Young President's Organization (YPO) meeting. I was very careful to dress in a conservative blue, three piece suit with freshly shined shoes. After my presentation, I was complimented on my tie by one of the attendees. I fortunately chose a foulard to wear. As I looked around the room, I noticed most of the YPO attendees also wearing foulards. I immediately understood the basis of the compliment. I was praised because I wore the same tie as the rest of them. People trust those who are like themselves both in behavior as well as in dress.

*The Club Tie*

A tie with repeating figures evenly spaced across it on a solid backbround is called a club tie. The figures are usually such things as sailboats, tennis racquets, ducks, or even corporate logos. It is typically an upper middle class tie reserved for those who may have a common interest. When I spoke to the Century 21 Corporation, not only did the men wear ties with repeating Century 21 logos, but everyone wore gold jackets as well. You are sure to create interest in your client or prospect by wearing a tie featuring figures that appeal to him. Unfortunately, if your tie has tennis rackets on it and your client's idea of exercise is watching Hulk Hogan wrestle on TV, you won't make any extra points. In fact, most professionals would rather make their products or services the topic of conversation instead of their tie. Speaking to a group of insurance agents in New Jersey, I sported an "I love New

Jersey" tie. It was an instant hit. I found immediate acceptance. However, if the group did not have that common New
Jersey interest, I would have diminished rapport. You can
imagine the reception I would have received if I wore that tie
to a program in New York.

## The Polka Dot Tie

The polka dot should be your most formal business tie. The
most traditional model is evenly spaced white dots on a navy
blue background. As you know, there are many variations.
The most coordinated look is to wear a tie with dots that pick
up the color of your shirt. Since the most common polka dot
tie is one with white dots, it tends to be the most conservative
look when worn with a white shirt. One rule to remember is
that the smaller the dot, the more formal the tie. If you have
a polka dot tie with dots the size of quarters, you may be wise
to wear it with a pair of outdated bell bottom trousers, and
only at home.

I once attended a financial planning conference at which
another speaker wore a formal polka dot tie with a sports coat
and slacks. After the speech, an attendee told me that something about his appearance distracted her. The speaker was
probably unaware of the conflicting image he was giving his
listeners. If you wear a polka dot tie with formal small dots,
dress in a conservative dark suit. This elegant neck piece is
most appropriate for dinner parties and formal receptions.
You'll make a good impression on both business associates
and friends when you wear this tie with the proper clothing
combination.

## The Solid Tie

The best tie to have in a limited wardrobe is a solid color tie.
It works with most garments to complete your wardrobe.
You should have both navy and maroon shades. Gray and

brown are optional solid tie colors. While not as conservative or formal as polka dot and foulard ties, the solid color tie should work well when selling to the lower middle class. It goes well with striped shirts and more casual clothes. It is also a safe tie to wear with a sports coat and slacks. These types of ties are typically worn by retail, over-the-counter salespeople.

While the solid tie is appropriate with more casual attire, you may lose an air of sophistication if you wear it with upper income clients. Of course, the opposite could also occur. You could intimidate your lower income clients by wearing a foulard or polka dot. I once sat next to a rock singer on an airline flight. He wore his conservative traveling clothes that day. His shirt was striped purple with a dark blue solid tie.

## WHY TIE PATTERNS MATTER

There is nothing magical about tie patterns and your overall dress with clients. No set rules will ever work all of the time. The basis for the appropriateness of foulard versus striped ties, for example, depends solely on the associations made by your client. Executives in financial industries have grown to expect fellow colleagues to dress conservatively in grays and blues, with neat hairstyles. Those in the recording industry expect each other to wear more casual and flamboyant types of attire. When an individual differs in dress from the norm, he is thought of as less trustworthy, a little strange or even eccentric. Through the years, these mores have been entrenched into an unspoken tradition, not soon changed. But, when someone who has "made it," like Lee Iacooca, with his striped shirt and solid white collar, or author Tom Wolfe, with his vintage all white suits, or even scientist Linus Pauling with his professorial bow tie, takes on a new look, others follow. We expect professors to wear bow ties. We expect educated upper class professionals to wear foulards. We expect the middle to lower middle class to wear solids and so on it goes in the world of business fashion.

I once flew on an airline to New York City. I wore a solid red tie with a line pattern button-down shirt. I was in possession of a first class ticket. After I found my seat, stowed my briefcase, and started reading the inflight magazine, a flight attendant walked over and said, "I'm sorry sir, this is first class. Can I see your ticket?" When she saw my seating assignment, she apologized. She said, "I'm sorry. But you didn't look like you should be up here."

The next time you pick a tie, remember that it could have a bearing on the level of rapport you gain with your prospect or client. Wearing the right tie at the right time may give you an edge in developing rapport more quickly. People develop rapport with those who are like them in both appearance and behavior. When we create rapport with others, we also create trust. When we establish trust, we are likely to establish a mutually beneficial business relationship.

The right tie can be a hidden persuader in making a sale. We'll discuss other hidden persuaders in the next chapter.

# PART 12

# HIDDEN PERSUADERS

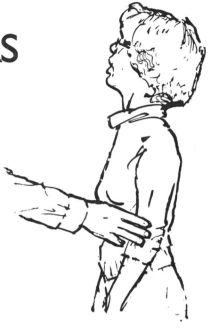

As I travel throughout the world speaking for top organizations, I am frequently approached by extremely successful salespeople. Many of these producers make in excess of two to three million dollars per year in commissions. Whether they are in real estate, insurance, stock brokerage, or own their own businesses selling widgets, these individuals frequently ask the same question, "Kerry, how do I get people to pay attention to what I have to say to them? We have changing products. We have diffcrent ways to finance paying for our products. In fact, with the new economic structures and taxation rules, many of our prospects and clients do not even know what to pay attention to, let alone know what to focus on specifically." They often say, "Kerry, I'd like to know a way of getting folks to understand more, to retain more, and remember more." Here's a quick question for you. Would you like to get your prospects and clients to understand three times as much in one half the time? I hope you said, "yes." In this chapter, you will learn how to increase the amount of information your prospect remembers and retains, and also how to raise your closing rate.

## A TOUCH OF PERSUASION

Two psychological researchers at the University of Minnesota at Minneapolis did a project a couple of years ago. The two researchers took an American twenty-five cent coin into a telephone booth, placed it on the ledge inside and walked out of the phone booth. Hiding behind a nearby tree, they waited for an unsuspecting subject to walk into the phone booth, pick up the quarter, and walk out with it. At that point, one of them approached the subject and said, "Did you happen to see my quarter in there? I left it in the phone booth. I need to make another telephone call." What would you say in this situation, "Yes or no?" If you thought, "No, I would keep it and not tell anyone where it came from," you would be in the vast majority. Only 23 percent of the subjects who were asked for the quarter actually gave it back. Twenty-three percent. Startling, isn't it? But these researchers, very bright individuals, did something else in the same project. For the second part of the study, they took another quarter, put it on the ledge inside the telephone booth, walked out, and again hid behind a tree. But in this case, they changed their approach in one critical way. They touched each unsuspecting subject below the elbow for not longer than three seconds and said, in effect, the same thing. "Sir, did you happen to see my quarter in that phone booth? I need to make another telephone call." In the second case, when the subjects were touched, the majority reached in their pockets and said something like, "I've been looking for someone to give this back to."

Now think back over the past twenty-four hours. Did you, in that time, touch somebody on the side of the arm to grab their attention, reinforce a comment, or underline a concept you wanted them to remember? You probably did. Do you realize you're doing this naturally, on your own? Why not make this a deliberate tool you can use to help your prospects remember and retain more and close them more quickly. Try this test. Walk up to a friend or aquaintance. Say something nice to them such as, "I like that sweater," or, "Your hair looks good today." After you give that compliment, say it one more time and simultaneously touch your friend below the elbow for not longer than three seconds. Go do that right now, and then come right back to this book. Which one worked better? Well, if you're like most people, your subject probably said that touching made a tremendous difference in how sincere they thought you were.

In fact, while speaking at a very large conference in Los Angeles, California, one gentleman, after hearing this, raised his hand in the middle of the program, stood up and said, "Kerry, I heard you speak about a year and a half ago. Soon afterward, I used this technique during a sale, to make a very important point with my prospect." He said, "I was with a female prospect, whom I had been talking with for over an hour. At the point I wanted to close, I touched her below the elbow on the side of the arm and told her I thought she should do as I had suggested and take advantage of the opportunity right now. At that very moment, the woman proceeded to reach in her purse, pull out her checkbook, and write me a check for the total amount of the purchase." Not only was the salesperson able to give greater impact to a key point, but he also closed in half the time that it normally would have taken him.

You may be thinking that some of your prospects or clients just don't like to be touched, and you're hesitant to try such a technique. Let me give some research findings to help you with this concern. Your prospects and clients may never know that they've been touched if you do it the right way. You've probably been in a library before, haven't you? If you were like most people in college, you probably checked a book out of the library. You handed the book to the librarian, and she scowled at you, as some librarians will do (it's too bad they're not paid on a commission). Did it ever seem to you as if those librarians never wanted to let you have the book in the first place? They were really giving the book to you under duress.

Well, the librarian would typically take your book and stamp the return date in it. She would then give the book back to you, saying something like, "Bring it back in two weeks or I'll break your legs." Do you remember those days?

After several of these episodes, one graduate student decided to take matters into his own hands. He got permission to conduct an experiment that revolutionized his college's library book return rate. He had the librarians treat a batch of students in their usual manner. At a certain point in the day, however, he had them make one minor change in their routine. As a student reached for the book, the librarian would touch him below the elbow for less than three seconds, and say basically the same thing, "Bring it back in two weeks or I'll break your legs." As you might have guessed, all those students were asked outside the library what they thought of the librarian. A significant number of the students who had been touched reported the librarian as being more sincere, persuasive, caring, warm, and smiling than the students who had not been touched. But the shocking result of the study showed that only 5 percent of the students who were touched, actually realized they had been contacted. Your prospect or client may never realize that he or she has been touched if you do it in the right way, below the elbow for not longer than three seconds.

You are probably wondering why below the elbow and certainly, why three seconds? During this study, they also discovered that if you touch a stranger above the elbow, you're basically penetrating very intimate distance and space. The area below the elbow, however, is considered a public space in which a total stranger can walk up to you, extend his or her hand, and shake yours. This is acceptable behavior from people we don't know very well. So, unless you want to risk becoming too intimate too quickly, make sure that you use this technique only below the elbow, not above. You will know you've violated the three second rule when you touch your prospect on the arm, and suddenly your prospect stares at your hand on his arm. This is clear, nonverbal communication that says, "Take your hand off me." You will probably never see this happening because of the simple fact that if you pay attention to timing, your prospect will never realize that he's been touched.

Nearly every salesperson and professional who has used this technique say that it works. If you touch your prospect or client on the arm below the elbow for less than three seconds to illustrate key ideas, you will obviously get them to remember more, retain more, and be more easily closed. But be careful. Don't keep touching that prospect. Try to hammer in the most key points that you want that person to remember. If you touch him too often, you may simply dilute the effectiveness of this very powerful technique. Touch your prospect from time to time, and you'll become more persuasive and be perceived by him as warmer and more sincere.

## YOUR BEST SIDE

There is also evidence that people retain some information much longer than others, depending on where they see it. This startling new evidence indicates that not only do your prospects retain information they see in certain areas longer, but you may even have a better side to your face.

University of Oregon researchers have now determined that people tend to retain more information they see in their right visual field than they do in their left visual field. This is especially interesting in light of the fact that everybody wonders which half of their face is their best side. It may have a lot to do with which side is more clearly remembered. As your prospects or clients look at you, the side of your face they see in their right visual field is the one they typically remember best and probably the side that most pleases them. So the best side of your face is your left side, not your right, because it is in your prospect's right visual field. This is fascinating when you think of what your prospect may retain and remember as you talk to him about your product. This research now shows that your prospect may retain three times as much of what he sees in his right visual field as he does in his left. This means that if you make your notes and illustrations on the right of the sheet, he may remember more of that than what he sees on the left side of the sheet. This is important to consider, because you probably are in the habit of putting all your notes on the left side margins. However, if you circle and highlight key ideas on the right side, you may make a bigger impact.

## THE TWELVE WORDS

Yale University researchers have also found certain key ideas that your prospect may understand better, retain, and remember longer. These very successful psychological researchers have found that there are certain words which your prospect likes to hear above all other words in the English language. These certain words, when used in direct mail, will actually increase response rates, be retained longer, and also, when linked with key ideas, increase the retention of ideas connected to the words. In fact, Madison Aveune is using these words in radio and television advertising. It's time we used these twelve most persuasive words with prospects. They are: 1) *Discovery*. Sears, Roebuck Corporation has a new credit card. Do you know what it is called? You got it, the Discover card! Did you really think that one of their vice-presidents said, "Hey guys, this is my favorite word. Why not call our credit card Discover?" They did years of research on which words carry the highest impact. 2) *Easy*. This will be easy for you. You will have absolutely no trouble, it's a cinch. 3) *Guarantee*. I guarantee this or your money back. It'll work; I'll stake my reputation on it. I guarantee it will be effective for you. 4) *Health*. Obviously, most of your prospects and clients care more about their health than they do about their money, and for good reason. If we lose our money, we can get it back. Regaining health is much more difficult. 5) *Love*. Video dating services are the matchmakers of our modern day, replacing the well-meaning mother-in-law who tried to help people fall in love more quickly. Many other industries play upon the appeal of love, including the wine and alchoholic beverage industries, florists, and candy makers. This is a key concept, a multi-million-dollar business based on helping people find love. 6) *Money*. Most people, as research reports, would have trouble paying off an unexpected bill of $1,000.00. You can bet that money ranks among the top three on this list. 7) *New*. In the United States, we have a strange preference for those things which are new as opposed to those which are old. We want the state of the art, "cutting edge," products. We cast away major items such as used cars and computers after short periods of time. We call them obsolete whether they work or not. We always want the latest model, the newest design. 8) *Proven*. We Americans have a strong desire to avoid things which are unproven and are not reliable. We want products that work that we won't have to take a chance on. 9) *Results*. The quickest way to get attention from your prospect is to let him know that what you sell him will get him results. It will work quickly and have a startling impact. 10) *Safety*. Very closely linked to health, safety is a characteristic of products that most people take for granted. 11) *Save*. Americans love discounts. They love getting a deal which they don't think anybody else will get. Even a deal that will not help them make money must at least help them save money. My grandmother, as I remember, often went to sales and bought articles just because she was saving money. It didn't matter whether she needed them or not, she was at least saving cash. 12) *You*. You will find this word peppered throughout this book. This is one of the most soothing words to your prospect's ear. The other, and even more soothing word, is your prospect's own name.

These words will help you put more persuasive zing into your communications. Use these words in brochures, and also when booking an appointment on the telephone. When you use these words during a telephone conversation, you'll cause your prospect to become more intent on what you're saying. They'll rivet their attention on whatever idea you're using in conjunction with these words.

These concepts, touching below the elbow, writing on the right side of the sheet, and the twelve most persuasive words, will all work if you utilize them. Such techniques will help you get an inside edge in communicating with your prospects and clients so that your successes will be far greater than you've experienced in the past. Use these tools, and you can look forward to increasing your sales immediately.

The next section deals with ways of getting prospects to buy. The first step, detailed in the following chapter, will show you how to recognize the signals a buyer may be giving you.

---

# HOW TO GET PEOPLE TO BUY

# PART 13

# BUYING SIGNALS

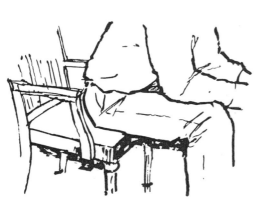

Recently, a very bright and articulate salesperson presented the perfect product to a qualified and interested prospect. Kevin, the prospect, had been referred to John, the salesman, by a mutual friend. In fact, the referral was so strong that John skated through the approach/rapport phase of the sales cycle. He discovered, during the probing phase of their conversation, that Kevin had a great need for his product. John presented his product masterfully. He tailored each feature exactly to Kevin's needs. John was really proud of the technical expertise he displayed during the presentation, Unfortunately, John kept talking, and talking . . . and talking until Kevin looked anxiously at his watch. He cut short the interview on the premise that he had another appointment scheduled.

What went wrong? John was a great prober/presenter. There is, however, another stage to a sale. No money is made unless you can *Close*. No commissions will fall into your pocket unless you are able to read your prospect's *buying signals*.

Have you ever oversold? Have you ever talked your prospect right into. . . and out of. . . a sale? Here is a sentence that will double or triple your business this year if you apply it:

## SELL YOUR PRODUCT
## WHEN YOUR PROSPECT WANTS TO BUY IT.
## NOT WHEN YOU WANT TO SELL IT!

As obvious as this may seem, research has shown that up to 30 percent of all sales are lost because the salesperson didn't know *when* to close. Knowing *When*, is as, or more, important as knowing *How*. Sales psychologists believe that every single behavior your prospect displays gives you information you can use to close in a sale. The following information will help arm you with the ability to recognize *When* your prospect wants to buy.

### HEAD NOD AND SMILE

The most basic of buying signals that even beginners will recognize are a smile and a "yes" head-nodding motion. Although this does not necessarily mean that a prospect will buy at that precise moment, this behavior pattern is an indication that the prospect is ready to buy, especially if it is more pronounced than when he first entered the room. But did you also know that the faster your prospect nods his head, the more he's thinking, "I wish this salesman would shut up!" The prospect is simply indicating through the nod, "I've heard this all before. Move on before I start to get bored." At this moment, the prospect should be asked, "I sense this is pretty familiar to you. Where have you heard it before?" Proud to display his knowledge, your prospect will clue you in on what he already knows (*listen* carefully because he may give you his *hot buttons*).

## PUPIL DILATION

While the head nod is probably obvious to you, this next buying signal may be new. Extensive video-taped interviews indicate that when nude photos are shown, the viewer's pupils will expand due to excitement and enthusiasm. You might be thinking, "Kerry, I don't get close enough to my prospect to see his pupils." You ought to. A majority of your prospects, no matter what the light level, will involuntarily display pupil dilation when they are highly enthusiastic about your ideas.

Do you remember the expression on your children's faces at Christmas time? They came out of their rooms and said, "Mommy, Daddy, is that for me?" Their eyebrows rose in gleeful joy. Did you ever see their eyes get round as saucers as their pupils dilated with pleasure?

Have you ever played poker? If you have, you may have noticed someone at that poker table wearing sunglasses. The guy wearing sunglasses had a full house! His pupils grew to the size of Firestone 500 tires.

Aristotle Onassis, the late Greek shipping tycoon, was rumored to always wear sunglasses during heavy business negotiations. If he didn't have his sunglasses, he would postpone his business meeting until he found a pair. He would also, conversely, refuse to negotiate a deal if his adversary was wearing sunglasses.

Is pupil dilation important? You bet. Unfortunately, Americans are not taught to notice such nuances. One of the reasons Russians often best us in arms negotiations is that they are taught to pay attention to such behavioral nuances they believe are windows to inner emotions.

## BUYER'S POSSESSIVENESS

One of the most sophisticated buying signals is how your prospect shows ownership with handouts and illustrations. Do you give your prospect illustrations to look at during a presentation? Watch what he does with it after he looks at it. Your prospect may glance over the sheet of paper and set it down. He may return it to your side of the conference table or even push it away. If he does one of these behaviors, he is showing psychological dispossessiveness. He is signaling to you, "The idea is not very impressive. My trust in you is low. I don't buy it." If you see this non-verbal cue, you may wish to go back to the probing stage. Find out his real need and/or desire. Don't even try to close yet. On the other hand, he may look at an illustration for a few moments. Then he may lay the sheet on his side of the table or desk. He may even clutch it and say, "Is this my copy?" His message is obvious.

I once went on an appointment with an inexperienced salesperson. During the presentation stage, the prospect was given a fact sheet. He immediately drew it closer to his chair. He was enormously possessive of the sheet and kept it without asking for a copy. To my amazement, the salesperson continued the presentation for more than forty-five minutes.

I saw the prospect go from moderate interest, via his buying signals, to apathy. I watched that salesperson, in the course of one hour, take his prospect in and back out of a sale. If you don't close your prospect at the right time, you'll buy your product right back.

## CHIN RUBBING

One of the most intricate buying signals is that of stroking or rubbing the chin. During the process of evaluation, most pros-pects will show some nonverbal sign indicating they are in deep thought. One will scratch his head while another may tense his lips. The most overt of these decision signals is the chin rub.

If your prospect does this be-havior, *stop talking immediately.* Your buyer is deciding whether or not to buy. If you keep talk-ing, you'll only serve to confuse and intimidate him. If you see this nuance, stop talking, simply wait for a few seconds, and pull out your contract to sign. Of course, he may give you an objection after he stops rubbing his chin. But you'll be sur-prised how many of your prospects will say yes at this point, and all because you knew when to stop talking.

## WHISTLING TEAPOT AND SITTING TREMOR BUYING POSITIONS

The most common buying signal your prospect will display is the position in which he sits. Through numerous hours of video playback, we have noticed an intriguing relationship between the way your prospect sits and his level of interest.

139

Most great salespeople understand that a prospect who sits back in his chair, with his arms folded and legs crossed, may not be very receptive. But when that same prospect moves forward or sits on the edge of his chair, the whistling teapot position, you've got the sale.

An even more dramatic buying position than the whistling teapot is the sitting tremor signal. It is also depicted by leaning

forward or sitting on the edge of a chair. But in this case, the prospect has one hand on his knee and the other forearm on his thigh. These people may be so enthusiastic to buy, they look as though they are about to explode any moment.

When I recently spoke at a sales conference in Edmonton, Alberta, Canada, I made the mistake of admitting that I was a guest speaker at a conference to Canadian immigration officials. Unfortunately, the officials detained me for over four hours the night I arrived. They insisted I was taking jobs away from Canadian citizens. The Sales Conference program chairman, who joined me in the immigration inspector's office, became increasingly hostile. I finally convinced the inspector that a speaker on sales psychology who was a pro tennis player would be difficult to replace with a Canadian. Leaning back in her chair, in the sitting tremor position, the inspector finally decided not to deport me. It was precisely at that moment that my host decided to give the inspector a piece of his mind. The inspector's next move was to slide back into her chair with her arms and legs crossed. It took me two more hours of negotiating to convince her again to let me stay in the country.

It is probably safe to say that even if you probe and present effectively, you won't make money unless you can close. Knowing *when* to close may make you more money than knowing *how*. Let your prospect buy when he's ready instead of when you are.

Craig Beachnaw, a top-producing salesperson in Lansing, Michigan, almost missed one of the biggest sales of his career. His prospect, a successful business owner, seemed to be giving buying signals. Craig determined his prospect's needs the first day. The second day Craig presented his product. An hour into the presentation, the owner moved into the sitting tremor position. Craig remembered my video program on buying signals and decided to stop talking. Craig pulled the sales agreement out and used a simple assumptive close. His prospect signed it immediately and smiled. Craig took him out to dinner that night and asked him why he said yes so quickly. The prospect said that he was ready to buy thirty minutes before Craig stopped talking. He admitted that Craig was actually talking him out of the sale. Craig was buying his product back!

If you watch for your prospect's buying signals, you'll close at least 30 percent more business. The million-dollar producers all admit that knowing *when* to close is as important as knowing *how*.

Women sometimes have particular problems in sales and marketing. In the next chapter we discuss these problems and some techniques to overcome them.

# PART 14

# HOW WOMEN CAN WIN IN SALES

Arlene, a bright and attractive salesperson, called a referred lead for an appointment. Following a short discussion on the telephone, the prospect readily agreed to the appointment. During the interview, Arlene sensed her prospect was holding back. He answered questions superficially and avoided giving her details regarding his situation. When she returned the next day for a presentation, her prospect was very cordial and polite but didn't buy her product. Following her presentation, he asked Arlene if she had a male associate.

Arlene may have been a victim of gender-related sales bias, a sort of sexual harassment in reverse. Many saleswomen, coast to coast, complain that their problems in sales differ greatly from those of men. The male sales population find that one of the most difficult aspects of selling is getting in the door. Once they get in, everything else is easy.

Women, on the other hand, often find it easy to successfully prospect. Their difficulty lies in generating a sufficient level of trust and respect, not only in prospecting activity, but also in presenting and closing. Without trust and respect, people will not buy, no matter how good the product.


## BRAINS VERSUS BEAUTY

Women must overcome several issues inherent in their gender. First, they may be "too pretty" for the prospect. A long-held myth states that men are intimidated by stunning beauty. That belief may be a major influence in business relationships as well as in courting behavior.

According to psychological researchers reporting in the *Journal of Personality and Social Psychology*, "good looks can actually hinder your success, if you're a woman." Research scientists used corporate business ID cards with photos to depict successful business people. These ID cards were sorted into groups such as homely, comely, male, and female. Researchers then showed these photos to businessmen and women who were asked to rate the photographs in terms of ability, luck, effort, political sophistication, and personal relationships.

Luck was most commonly cited as the reason for goal achievement in unattractive men who were successful in business. In contrast, ability was attributed to the success of unattractive women. When attractiveness was a striking characteristic, results were markedly different. Attractive men were thought to possess a high level of ability that contributed to their success. Surprisingly, attractive women were thought of as possessing less ability in job performance than unattractive women. Good-looking women were seen as less capable than their not-so-attractive sisters. This finding is familiar to those who understand social relationships. A dumb blond is known as "a pretty blond female who has an IQ below room temperature." Such attitudes are a major reason women sometimes have difficulty gaining respect from prospects.

## IS IT BAD TO BE BEAUTIFUL?

Why the reluctance to attribute professional acumen to attractive women? Psychological researchers concluded that highly successful business people needed to possess masculine skills. Attractive men were automatically seen as more masculine. In contrast, beautiful women were regarded as especially feminine and less likely to possess successful masculine business skills. When attractive women make it in business their success is often seen as a fluke.

In addition to attractiveness, women have a second obstacle to overcome in selling to men. They often have a more difficult time communicating with males than other men do.

## SMALL TALK

*Vogue* magazine reports that as children, boys and girls play in sex-separate groups. They learn patterns of communication from their peers. Girls tend to have a female best friend who becomes the center of her social life. They do a lot of talking together, placing value on being polite and supporting each other's feelings, as well as sharing secrets. Their relationship revolves around the discussion of the details of their lives. Boys do not socialize in the same way. Their focus is on outdoor activities, usually in large groups. They don't put value on communicating their emotions. To boys, talk itself becomes competitive. Telling jokes and stories are their way of maintaining the center of attention. Girls want to be popular but avoid attracting too much attention.

Communication gaps arise when boys and girls grow up continuing these patterns as adults. Women often become dissatisfied and frustrated in close relationships with men because their lover or husband does not function as their best friend. Women want to discuss their innermost emotions, fears, and problems. They may even talk about their feelings toward other people. Men tend to communicate much more pragmatically. The little details of what they do all day seem unimportant to relate.

Women are often described as roundabout in their communication. They may believe that an indirect approach pays off in developing healthy rapport. For them, it is best to be understood without saying what they mean, or to get what they want without asking for it. When it comes to a relationship, they may think, "Why, after all these years, do I have to tell you what I mean or what I want?" And men think, "What kind of a relationship do we have? Can't you just tell me plainly what you want?" Both are equally reasonable. However, it's not a matter of sense or reason; it's an issue of upbringing.

## SUCCESSFUL WOMEN

Most working women who are successful have a combination of masculine and feminine communication styles. Although they do possess many of the same business duties as men, they are able to maintain their feminine characteristics. A man might *tell* his secretary to type a letter, while a woman may politely *ask* if he or she would do the same task.

Due to these differences, women often have a tough time closing a prospect. A man often is more direct in his close than a female. He may use an assertive *alternate of choice* or even an *implied consent* close. The woman, on the other hand, may be less willing to close directly. She may be inclined to put greater emphasis on a polite relationship with a prospect. A woman may, more than a man, fear losing rapport if a prospect does not respond to a direct close. She could even fail to make a sale because she waited for the prospect to close himself, a rare occurrence at best.

Women are caught in a dilemma. If they behave as a female, response to their sales techniques may be negative. If they behave as men, their femininity rating may drop drastically. Geraldine Ferraro is a perfect example of this predicament. In her role as a politician, she was very assertive, and during her vice presidential campaign she conducted herself like any other candidate. As a result, she was regarded as a harsh, domineering female.

## WHAT WORKS FOR WOMEN

Women may have an easier time selling to other women than to men. Simply being armed with the knowledge that they may have a tougher time will prepare them for the rejection that could ensue. Indeed, the feminine/masculine communication differences may actually help rather than hinder women.

One advantage is that women generally have an easier time getting in the door than men. Women may also be more adept at probing because of their enhanced ability to build relationships. However, the presentation stage demands a more direct masculine communication style. For example, when answering objections, the female may feel compelled to avoid a perceived conflict. Instead, she should use the male style of challenging the prospect by saying, "Why is this important to you?"

In closing, the female can also incorporate the male's style of directly asking for the order. She would be wise to avoid an indirect close in favor of a straightforward, "Let's get this going now" assertion.

## SALES SUPERSTARS

One application for women is doing a trial close after answering an objection. A businesswoman might feel the threat of conflict when an objection is presented. She may attempt to avoid the duress of the objection by answering it unassertively, and instead strive to preserve the relationship she so carefully cultivated. The problem is she may not be able to close at the best time possible, directly after an objection has been made. For example, Joy, on my staff, was given an objection by one of our prospects. The program chairman said, "Kerry is over-exposed in our city. We don't want him back any sooner than five years." Joy said, "I understand that you think he's over-exposed. In fact, when he spoke in Boston last year, more people attended than in any previous year. The attendance numbered 765 because so many who previously heard Kerry speak returned with their associates. Would you like Kerry to speak before or after lunch?" Joy assertively closed the prospect using a direct masculine technique. She said later it felt a little heavy-handed, but it worked. It may have seemed heavy to her but not to the prospect.

A second way women can optimize the male/female communication differences is to effectively use the "implied consent" and "alternate of choice" closes. In viewing how women sell, I have observed them practically making the prospect beg to buy. Most prospects will not do this. They'll just end the interview. Instead, they should be more assumptive. As soon as she has presented an idea, the successful woman, should immediately pull out the product contract. If the prospect doesn't stop her from filling in the contract with an order, the sale is completed. It works because many prospects do want to buy, but they won't tell the salesperson. Sales will increase by 30 percent overnight with this technique. The alternate of choice close again simply lets the prospect buy without saying yes. He is given a choice of two alternatives, "Mr. Prospect, we discussed some possible solutions to help you achieve your financial objectives. Would you rather have a 9 percent taxable fund or the 8 percent tax-free fund?" Many women would feel uncomfortable with this type of direct close. I recommend that women role-play for at least an hour with a manager or associate to practice these direct approaches to closing.

## THE BEST OF BOTH WORLDS

Businesswomen can have the best of both worlds in effective selling if they recognize the differences between feminine and masculine communication styles. They can outperform males in sales if they study carefully how men sell, and then incorporate male styles into their overall presentation and closing strategies. Women have bigger roadblocks to overcome in selling than men, but they also have a much greater potential for becoming sales superstars!

The telephone has become one of the most valuable tools. In the next chapter, we shall study effective telephone marketing techniques.

# PART 15

## HOW TO GET TRUST ON THE TELEPHONE

Recently I was prospected on the telephone by a salesperson representing a major company. She started by saying, "Mr. Johnson?" "Yes" "Mr. Kerry Johnson?" "Yes. . ." As she read her thirty second approach script, my attention started to drift. This telephone salesperson was possibly the worst cold call telemarketer I have heard. She read a script designed to attract one or two prospects out of 100 calls. A direct mail solicitation would have been more effective. Those granting her an appointment probably had $10 a month of disposable income or thought she was connected with a "Publishers Clearing House" giveaway program. If she had used just a few of the techniques you are about to learn, she could have made a minimum of seventy to eighty appointments for every 100 telephone calls.

The Dartnell Institute reports that the cost of seeing a prospect face-to-face has passed the $200 mark. Counting travel and preparation time, as well as staff support hours, this figure seems realistic. According to Shelby Carter, senior vice-president with Xerox Corporate sales, "windshield time" needs to be reduced and "contact time" needs to be increased. And yet, if you're like me, you still receive numerous letters containing information that could more easily be communicated by phone.

In our contemporary business world, if you're good on the telephone, you will substantially increase your income. One sales producer I know, who is with a real estate limited partnership company in California, has a sales territory of six states, yet he travels only two days per week. He's number one in production in his company. This is surprising when you think that his competitors travel five to six days each week, rarely seeing their families. A Smith-Barney stockbroker in Southern California earns $750,000 each year. He has met only 1/3 of his clients in person. Of that 1/3, he has seen only 10 to 20 percent a second time. Yet, he keeps in touch constantly.

Are you good on the telephone? If your face-to-face closing rate is less than 75 to 80 percent, there's room for improvement. For those of us in face-to-face sales, telephone effectiveness means approaching and qualifying so skillfully that when you eventually do meet in person, the sale is guaranteed. You are not an amateur, you don't need to practice. But, how do you get good on the telephone?

Unfortunately, many salespeople have little or no training in telephone sales skills. Most companies are more concerned with product training, rather than with professional telephone techniques. One copier salesperson I interviewed recently said, "I've been selling for five years and never received training on how to sell on the telephone. I'd love to improve my average of two appointments out of ten phone calls." Not only will your number of appointment bookings increase from telephone calls, but you will increase your closing rate on face-to-face appointments. Here are a few tips designed to help you decrease "windshield time" and increase production.

## GETTING THROUGH TO THE PROSPECT

If you've been in sales for more than a few weeks and have an I.Q. above room temperature, you already know the power of a good referral. If it is strong, meaning the prospect knows and respects the source of the referral, you've got an attentive audience. If the referral is weak, you are practically making a cold call. One of the best ways of approaching a referral is to first find out something about them. A referral is effective because you are making use of a strong social bond between two people. If you can also form a bond between you and your prospect, you'll develop trust on the telephone. When you develop trust, you will develop a sale.

The usual way to develop rapport and trust for most telephone salespeople is to say, "How are you?" Please take your pencil and write "How are you" 100 times across a sheet of 8 1/2 X 11 paper. When you're done, cross each phrase out. Never use these words on the telephone again. Even if your prospect is suffering from a 104 degree fever, he'll say, "Fine." Instead, use this three-step technique: 1) introduce, 2) state purpose of call, 3) develop rapport. This simple technique will make a good call even stronger and prevent a marginally interested prospect from hanging up on you.

Here's an example of introduce, purpose, and rapport. "Mr. Thomas? Hello, Mr. Thomas, my name is Kerry Johnson, John Jacobs and I had a short chat about you last week. I'm a financial planner with Marginal Equities Corporation in Los Angeles. John mentioned that you might be interested in exploring some possibilities of increasing your investment return. By the way, John tells me you're an excellent tennis player. Is that true?"

The sequence of these steps has an enormous impact. The most productive telephone salespeople in the nation know that if they can use their prospect's name two or three times during their initial approach, they'll involve him. The key to doing business on the telephone is to avoid speaking for more than fifteen seconds at a time. If you violate this rule, you'll allow the prospect to blow you off the call with quick objections. By saying hello after you introduce yourself rather than how are you, you'll enable the listener to give you a sincere greeting rather than a phony, "I'm fine." The objective is to develop personal rapport with that prospect. With people I know, I often say, "How is your day going?" This may seem like I'm saying the same "How are you" but the words are different although the meaning is the same. If you take your prospect out of his greeting rut, he'll respond to your rapport.

During step two, purpose, your primary goal is to give the prospect an opportunity to organize in his mind who you are and how you might be of service. If you instead go to the rapport phase, ahead of purpose, the prospect will become suspicious.

I made the mistake once of calling a referral, saying, "Mr. Thomas? Hello, Mr. Thomas, my name is Kerry Johnson. John Jacobs referred you to me. He says you're quite a tennis player. How long have you been playing?" I didn't get three more words out before the prospect said, "What do you want? Why are you calling?" Instead of generating rapport, I lost it. The prospect became suspicious. He wanted to know right away why I was calling. I neglected stating the purpose of my call before going to rapport.

Step three is the most important. This is the glue that holds a relationship together, even on the telephone. Assuming you've done a good job of preparation in learning something about your prospect, this is your chance to make him smile. Rarely do salespeople ask more than, "How's the weather there?" But when you let that prospect know that you've taken the time to learn something about him, you'll be darn near impossible to reject. Prospects reject *cold call cowboys,* not sincere referrals who know something about them already.

## RAPPORT

Let me give you an idea of how crucially important it is to develop a high degree of rapport on the telephone, before you try to do any business. I recently had a meeting scheduled with my attorney. I met my wife and accountant at the attorney's office, since we drove separately. Unfortunately I was detained, and was ten minutes late for the appointment. As I entered the attorney's office, he was already speaking. Unfortunately, I had never met him before. The attorney acknowledged me by shaking hands and saying hello, and then went right back into what he was discussing with my wife and accountant. I was so distracted by his appearance, the way he talked, the modulation of his voice, and his physical movements, that I really wasn't able to pay attention for the first few minutes of our conversation. Although the attorney was a very nice looking man, with no distracting qualities about him, I found it difficult to attend to his comments. It suddenly dawned on me how important it is to chat about personal common interests before business is conducted.

Think about it. Even on the telephone, if you jump right into business with somebody you don't know well, you're depriving yourself of learning what the prospect means instead of just what he says. You need to learn what they sound like, when they're excited or sad, interested or disinterested. But yet, if you are able to talk about baseball or football, as a way of establishing rapport, you are also able to find out what that person really means as he uses phrases, words, and unique speaking characteristics. This will then make your job much easier as you bridge into conducting business. The benefit of rapport is that it prepares you and your prospect for meaningful dialogue. Without that introductory rapport development, you will very likely miss most of what's really going on behind what's being said.

The question to ask at this point is, "How long should I stay in the rapport-building phase?" Even if you've got a busy prospect, you'll be surprised how long he wants to talk about his favorite subject, himself. Practice here what psychologists call pro-active listening. The more you can facilitate what a referral says, the more rapport you'll generate. I've often been asked, "How do I know when to jump back to business?" If you listen well, your prospect will let you know. Recently, I called a prospect who had not spoken to the referral for over a year. When I got through to the prospect, he was so brusque, I could feel sweat beading on my forehead. I could almost see, through the telephone line, his forefinger poised over the switchhook. After I introduced myself and stated the purpose of my call, I quickly interjected, "Don tells me you have a cabin in Banff. I've heard it's beautiful up there." My prospect was off to the races. I happened to mention that the cabin seemed like a great reward in life. He became so comfortable with me that he invited me up for a visit at the end of our conversation. I only spoke to him for ten to fifteen minutes. But instead of hanging up, he hung on. He did become a client, simply because our rapport level was high.

## GETTING THROUGH ON COLD CALLS

One of the most difficult calls to generate rapport is the cold call. By definition, it is a prospect you know almost nothing about personally. But yet, if you're smart enough, you can even motivate this prospect to generate rapport with you. Many salespeople send a mass mail letter out before they call. While it is a good strategy, most salespeople don't play upon the impersonal weakness of the letter. Instead of moving directly into asking your prospect questions say, "I bet you don't receive many direct mail letters like mine, do you?" He'll instantly laugh. He knows as well as you that he's up to his waist in junk mail every day. If you can interject humor into your call, the ice will break all over that telephone. Obviously, humor can backfire, but used sincerely, you'll generate business. Chances are that on cold calls, your chances of getting rejected are higher. If you use humor to generate rapport, you'll last longer and get more business to boot. Your prospect wants to feel good. Give him something to smile about. I once cold called a prospect in Oregon. I said, "My name is Kerry Johnson. I'm calling you from Southern California, one of the last areas in the country where you can still buy a $20,000 house for $1.2 million." He chuckled. We developed rapport. We did business. We both got what we wanted.

## THE THREE STEPS

Practice the three-step approach: 1) introduction, 2) purpose, 3) rapport. Whether you're on a cold call or in the midst of making a strong referral call, you'll win with rapport and lose without it.

I've been able to listen in during phone calling sessions with salespeople at numerous companies. One common characteristic all good telephone salespeople have is the ability to gain their prospects' trust by generating rapport on the phone. The salespeople reporting the greatest difficulty on the telephone thought they could get appointments by talking only about their products. If you're good on the phone, you'll prepare your prospect for an appointment that will be productive. It will be productive because he will look forward to seeing you. He will see you because you did more than just make a prospecting call. You earned trust.

## QUALIFYING: HOW TO REACH YOUR PERFECT PROSPECT

After you get rapport, you'll move into the probing phase of the interview. This is the stage in which you'll quickly determine if you're talking to a prospect who needs your product and has the resources to buy it. It's known as the *qualification* phase. Most good telephone salespeople early in their careers dial the telephone at least forty to fifty times per hour and often make as many as 150 to 200 calls per day. The really good ones spend no more than four to five minutes on a phone call. They continue talking to the prospect only if he shows some degree of initial interest.

Very sophisticated and sharp telephone salespeople know whether their prospect is someone to pursue. They use what's called a *trial close* bridged in the qualification. Many salespeople get right to the point as they qualify. One stockbroker I know talks about stock market opportunities for about thirty seconds to one minute. But then he quickly qualifies by saying, "Mr. Jones, if I found an investment idea that could return 30 percent or more per year, would you have any trouble investing $20,000 right now?" Sure there is always that chance that the prospect might lie. But barring that difficulty, if the prospect says, "Gee, I really don't have that kind of money lying around," then get off the telephone quickly. But if he says, "Sure, if it is a good product and could help achieve my goals, I guess I could get the money together," then you've got a good prospect.

It's important to qualify for money immediately after you present a benefit your prospect seems receptive to. In other words, don't qualify for money too early. You may scare your prospect. But after he receives some value or an idea of how your product will benefit him, then a qualification for money is very appropriate. Remember, don't give the cost of your product before the value is given. But, there's nothing stopping you from asking non-money qualification questions early on. In my company, we often ask a prospect in the first two or three minutes how many people will be at a meeting. If there are under a hundred, I will rarely negotiate my speaking fee. But if there's over a hundred people, I'm very motivated to adjust my price. On the other hand, if there's under twenty people, I may not do the program at all.

The perfect prospect for my business is someone we spend a lot of time tracking down. We know how many people work for him. We know his budget. We know his needs. We know what motivates him. When I find a prospect, I try to make sure that his business and psychological make-up is as close to the perfect prospect profile that I can get. That's how we qualify. Another way to qualify is the survey approach. This is especially effective in making cold calls. Since it's important to grab your prospect's attention in the first thirty seconds, asking survey questions will not grab him it will but give him something he likes to do. People love answering survey questions. They love to be involved in a survey that might be published somewhere. In fact, when I was at Walt Disney World in Orlando, Florida, I went on an attraction which was basically a glorified survey. All the hostess did was sit on a chair with a button, letting us look at television commercials. The line to get in the attraction was wrapped around the building.

Here's an example of a survey question to qualify. "Mr. Franks, I'm from TDY Communications. I'm not sure our telephone discount service can help you but I would like to ask you a couple of questions to find out. Which two cities do you call most often? How much is your overall monthly bill? How many people make long distance phone calls?" For this salesperson, if more than two cities are called it may not warrant discount rates. If the monthly bill is under $500, this may not be a good prospect. In an effort to save time, do not stay on the telephone.

Without qualifying effectively, you'll earn 20 percent of your dollars from 80 percent of your prospects. Qualifying will make sure you spend 80 percent of your time on 20 percent of the most productive prospects. You'll then make more money, more quickly.

If you are simply selling a product by phone or attempting to book an appointment, you'll be more successful by gaining trust and qualifying well before you move into any other phases of sales interaction.

*Listening* is one of the most misunderstood but most important facets of business communication. In the next chapter, we will explore what listening is, why we listen the way we do, and how we can improve our listening skills in gaining more business.

# PART 16

# "LISTEN" YOUR PROSPECT INTO BUYING

Think back, for a moment, about the past week. How many people can you remember who were good listeners, people who were not only attentive, but also remembered what you said! Chances are, you only met a couple of people in the last week you thought were good listeners. What were your feelings towards these few? You probably had feelings of comfort, trust, and likeability.

We are all very vulnerable to certain myths regarding listening. Salesmen think of themselves very often as being good talkers instead of good listeners. They may think of a sales superstar as having the "gift of gab. He is a born talker. What a promoter. Selling is telling or telling is selling. He sure is quick on his feet." Is the focus of these comments toward listening? No, it's on talking. Many people believe that speech is power and that listening is subservient. Just the opposite is true. A good listener has much more power in a conversation. He is able to glean more information than the speaker. In fact, when you think about a conversation between two people, who is really directing the discussion. Isn't it the person who asks the questions? Isn't it the listener? Over 50 percent of a salesperson's or manager's job revolves around listening. Successful and productive business people will agree. The Sperry Rand Corporation has obviously learned this too. Now, renamed Unisys, they have spent hundreds of thousands of dollars training their sales people in becoming better listeners. Their T.V. commercials advertised, "We have found that people just don't listen. We at Sperry are becoming better listeners. We are training secretaries and executives alike to listen in order to help you." These advertisements are aired coast to coast, especially after football games. They show their salespeople, managers, and support personnel in classrooms listening to their teachers talk *about* listening. You often see them tilting their heads and taking notes. They are very quiet, obviously paying attention. It is probably one of the most important commercials of this decade because this company tries to show the public that they care about their clients, that they are willing to listen and pay attention. This new advertising message takes advantage of the positive emotions we feel toward good listeners.

But business is not the only place that listening is important. Marriage counselors often back up the fact that couples break up not because of incapability or disagreements, but because of a lack of communication. I saw a movie recently about a couple who went to a marriage counselor because of strained marital relations. The counselor said, "Communicate better and your marriage will improve." He further said, "Listen to each other once in a while and you will be surprised at how much better your relationship will become." Well, the next morning after seeing that counselor, the husband was reading the morning paper. The wife was also reading another section of the paper about fashions. The husband blurted out, "Look at that, they won again! By three touchdowns! I've made a a few bucks on that game." The wife interjected, "A few bucks; look at the money I can save on this dress. If I can get down to Saks before one o'clock, I'll probably beat the crowd and get what I want. I can save a lot of money on that beautiful maroon dress that will go so nicely with my white jacket." The husband said, "Imagine, advertising coats in the sports section. Why don't they leave 'em out and just put football in it. Why do they have to let those dumb advertisements clutter up the section." Then the wife said, "Coats, look at that price. That jacket would look so good with my blue top and white belt. I've got to take advantage of this sale *today*." The husband put his paper down just as his wife was sipping her coffee. He said, "Isn't it incredible how well we communicate now?" Each was talking about two totally different subjects at the same time. How much of this do you do in speaking to your spouse or loved one? Do you really listen? No one is born with the ability to listen effectively. Just like all other communication skills, good listening must be learned. To a great extent this involves forming good listening habits and breaking bad ones.

## LEARNING TO LISTEN

In business, approximately 5 percent of your day is spent writing, 15 percent is spent reading, 30 percent of your day is spent talking, and 50 percent is spent listening. It is not surprising that so many of us are not good listeners. Most of us have spent at least twelve years in school. During that time we spent approximately half of our education learning to communicate, and of that time, 40 percent was spent reading, 35 percent writing, 25 percent talking and 0 to 1 percent learning how to listen. Much of that listening time was in the form of "be quiet Tommy and pay attention," or "if you don't listen, I will put you in the corner." A few years ago, the New York City Police Department did a study of the type of men who engage prostitutes. They found that over 36 percent of the males who went to prostitutes did so, not because they were mentally deranged or had psychological problems, but because they wanted someone to listen to them. They frequently would pay a prostitute her fee just to sit and listen.

## POWER LISTENING

Here are some techniques and tips that will allow you to become a better listener and an effective and efficient communicator.

*First, a good listener will repeat and clarify information.* A great deal of information is lost through one-way communication. For example, a boss gives you a command, "I want you to get this out by next Monday so see what you can do with it. Be sure it is double spaced and make it look professional to the client. Make sure, above all, that you include the price and let him know that we are going to do a good job for him." This is one-way communication. Information is lost because the listener is not participating or clarifying the message. This is common in sales and results in frequent misunderstandings. Two-way communication is much better. When someone makes a comment or request see what you can do with this proposal. Try to make it as exacting as possible, in two-way communication, the listener might say, "What exactly do you want me to do with it? When do you want it completed?" He will work with the speaker in trying to put the most information to use in the best way.

There is also a deeper facet of communication that is important in listening. It is called *congruency*. Congruency provides two-way communication through interaction between the speaker and the listener, because the listener learns to listen to the emotions to reach a point of trust with the speaker. Many of us in sales deal with the same types of people day in and day out. I met a real estate agent recently who told me about a couple who wanted to buy a house. The couple told the agent exactly what they wanted. However, the agent didn't adequately listen and consequently showed them something they did not like. After spending two weeks looking at the wrong kind of houses, the agent lost his client because he *assumed* they were like everybody else who wanted a three-bedroom, two-bathroom ranch-style home. In order to achieve congruency, a good listener will not only repeat and clarify information but also will summarize points at the end for the speaker. This lets the speaker know that you are paying attention and have reached the same understanding of the conversation as the speaker intended. A good listener will repeat and clarify information.

*Second, a good listener listens to a speaker at-tension.* During the stress workshops that I give, I teach that stress is usually measured on a bell shaped curve of 0 to 100, with 0 as a very relaxed state, almost asleep, and 100 as an anxiety state where some of us experience so much tension that we find difficulty even thinking logically. At 100 we also have trouble concentrating on work. Well, on this scale of 1 to 100, there is an area that is optimal in listening tension, the 30 to 40 level. This is where enthusiasm thrives. You feel good while there is just enough stress to cause us to produce and achieve. When we are at that level, we are able to assimilate a lot of information that we may put into future action. When we keep ourselves very attentive, our memory improves. A short time ago, an insurance agent told me that he would spend every Monday, Wednesday, and Friday morning on the phone, making referral calls. One day after about the twelfth call, he spoke to one man for a few minutes and found himself drifting off. It was brought abruptly to attention when the prospect said, "What do you think of that?" The agent replied,

"Oh right, I agree," even though he hadn't heard what the prospect said. This could prove to be a very embarrassing situation. A good way to keep yourself attentive, gain more information, and be a better listener is to keep alert and grip the edge of a chair or buy a gripper that body builders use to increase their gripping strength. Utilizing this exercise will in turn keep you attentive as a listener. Another suggestion you can use is to stand up. When you stand while you talk on the telephone you cause yourself to be more alert. Studies have shown that the more attentive and alert you are, the more information you will retain. When I was an instructor at the University of California, I would suggest ways for my students to prepare for examinations. I recommended that if they walk up and down the dormitory halls reading their notes, they would increase their memory retention and get better grades on tests. Stay attentive, keep yourself at that 30 to 40 stress level. A good listener listens to a speaker at-tension.

*Third, a good listener exchanges information.* Good salespeople know that you can't sell unless you find a need. You can't fill it unless you ask questions first about that need. But needs have to be uncovered. The way to uncover needs is knowing how to ask questions. A good listener knows this. He doesn't ask *too many* questions. He doesn't give the speaker a feeling of being pumped by asking a lot of questions, one right after the other. A short time ago, I was traveling from Long Island to New York City on a commuter train. I sat next to a man who was reading a newspaper. Across from me another man was looking out the window at the scenery. He then turned his gaze to the man with the newspaper and said, "Hey buddy, what's on the front page today?" The newspaper reader said, "Looks like the Jordanians are having verbal disputes with the Israelis, talking about the West Bank again. Of course the Egyptians are reaching an agreement in the Sinai and it looks like it will be good for Middle East peace." Then the other man said, "What about sports, how are the Knicks doing?" "Well, the Knicks lost last night and it also looks like the Jets have no chance in the playoffs this year." "What about economics?" "Well the prime rate is increasing another point and unfortunately it looks like we are going to have a housing crisis in the next six months." "Oh really, what about the current, fiscal financial crisis in New York City?" After that question was asked, the newspaper reader crackled his newspaper, then straightened it out and put it up between the person who was asking all the questions and himself. Can you imagine how you would feel if someone was machine gunning questions at you like that. It is important to give prospects, or anyone else you are speaking with, the reason why you want to know something. Simply give them past experiences. For example: If you tell them *what* you want to know and *why* you want to know it, your chances of getting the right information willingly from the speaker are greatly enhanced. You will also develop trust and empathy with the person you are asking questions of. So ask a question and then give some background information on it. You will avoid giving them the feeling of being pumped or interrogated. A good listener exchanges information.

*Fourth, a good listener adjusts to emotion-laden words.* We all have a holding tank of words that trigger emotions. These are words that cause us to stop listening and focus on a bad experience. Here are some words that may serve as examples to show you how distracting emotion-laden words can be. What do you think of when I mention inflation? or bills? cost of living? vacation? or how about interest rates? These are all words which conjure up intense feelings. They also tend to distract the listener.

Recently I saw an Abbott and Costello movie. Abbott was locked in a cell with a man who had a beard down to his waist and hair down to his shoulders. He was dressed in a tattered robe. He looked like he had been in a cell for twenty years and was obviously psychologically demented. Abbott watched his fellow prisoner staring out through the bars at the ocean. Abbott said, "Why am I here? I have done nothing wrong.

167

This is really going to spoil my vacation to Niagara Falls." The mad man broke his conversation on the ocean and said, "Inch by inch, slowly I turn, closer and closer," and proceeded to throw Abbott into the bars, against the wall of the cell, and beat him up. Abbott recovered and asked, "Why did you do that?" The madman said, "Do what? Let me help you up." He obviously had forgotten everything he had just done. Abbott said, "Boy, don't you ever do that again." The madman looked out the window again. Commiserating, Abbott said, "If only I could be in Niagara Falls, everything would be okay." Suddenly the madman went into his trance again and said "Inch by inch, slowly I turn, closer and closer;" and for the second time, proceeded to beat up Bud Abbott. Abbott again shook himself out of his stupor and said, "I *understand* now why you did that." The madman asked, "Did what?" Abbott replied, "Beat me up. I know why you did it. It's because I said..." The madman replied, "Said what?" Abbott said, "Oh no, I'm not going to say those words again." The madman said, "What words, what are you talking about." Abbott said, "You're not going to get me to say it *that* easy. Oh no." The madman said, "I don't know what you are talking about. What is this?" and Abbott said, "You're not going to get me to say *Niagara Falls.*" This triggered the madman to say, "Inch by inch, slowly I turn...." " This is an extreme example of emotion-laden words. A good way to avoid falling into the problems that these words bring is to empathize with the speaker as to the reason he is using the words. Listen to the usage of that word from *his* point of view, instead of reacting to it from your own. Avoid associations of your own emotions to his words.

I heard a story recently about a college coed who wrote a letter to her parents. Her father saw the envelope and said, "Boy, Donna doesn't write much, I wonder what she's written to us about. She probably wants money or has written to tell us she is getting bad grades." Well, the mother opened the letter and read it out loud to the father.

"Dear Mom and Dad, I just want to tell you that everything is ok and I love you both very much. But, there are a couple things I need to tell you. Something bad has happened. My roommate did so poorly on her midterms that she went up on top of the dorm building and jumped off, committing suicide. I can't tell you how upset I was and still am. I was so depressed that I had to quit my job. Because I'm not working, I lost my car. I couldn't make the payments. I am still shaken horribly over these things. Well, since I haven't got any money, I moved in with my boyfriend. I know how you feel about living with a man out of wedlock, Mom and Dad, but he is such a wonderful person. He does everything for me. He gives me so much. He doesn't even care that I am pregnant. He said, "Go ahead, have the baby, and I'll still love you." He is a wonderful person, Mom and Dad. He even said that he wouldn't go to the pool halls while I'm pregnant and gamble on billiards as he did before. He will even stay with me in the evenings. I realize that this may not be exactly what you want for me, but he said as soon as I have the baby, I can quit school and work to support the family."

You can imagine the shock the parents are feeling at this point. The letter goes on... "Mom and Dad, none of the things I have written about are true. I love you very much and miss you. I just wrote you to say I got a D in history and I need 100 bucks for a ski trip next month. Love, Donna." Did you hear all the emotion-laden words like pregnancy, living together, suicide? You can imagine what the parents focused on while reading the letter. If we are going to be good listeners, it is important to listen to the words that are being used from the speaker's point of view. A good listener adjusts to emotion-laden words.

*Fifth, a good listener hears the speaker out.* All of us intensely dislike being interrupted. We desire to express complete ideas. We all want to be heard and desire to say what we have on our mind. It disturbs all of us not to be able to complete an idea or express a whole opinion. Recently, a car salesperson who had previously heard me at one of my workshops on listening said, "Hearing a speaker out really does help. I met for three hours with a prospect and showed him the perfect affordable car of his dreams. He bought it. Two days later I called him back before I put the financial information through and the prospect said over the phone, "I'm glad you called. I have been thinking about this car and all the things we have talked about. I think that it isn't such a great idea for me to buy this at this time. I really haven't got the money for the monthly payments and I am not sure I am ready for it." The salesman felt like saying, *"Wait a minute. I spent three hours with you the other evening. We talked about definite benefits and advantages, ways to pay for this car with tax write-offs, let alone resale values. How can you say something like this?* You know it is the right move for you." But the car salesman remembered my seminar and avoided saying that. After attending my workshop he learned to let the speaker complete his ideas. The prospect went on to say, "Yes, I really can't afford it. But then again, I've worked hard. I deserve this car. And it *will* help with taxes. I think it is a good idea after all. I'll drop by and we'll complete this transaction."

How many times do we make mistakes by cutting in on a speaker, interrupting him before he has completed his thoughts. Find out what the speaker is trying to say first. When the time comes for you to respond to what he has said, let the speaker catch his breath before speaking. This gives the speaker the idea that you are not only listening but are also thinking about your response. *A good listener hears the speaker out.*

*Sixth, a poor listener listens to facts; a good listener listens to emotions.* Think of communication as an iceberg. Above water, the iceberg is facts. Theoretically, 20 percent of communication is strictly facts. 80 percent of that iceberg is emotion. The eighty percent down below the water line is the feelings and the emotions that we all have and put into every thought. If you are not listening to the whole iceberg in a conversation, you are missing 80 percent of what the person is really trying to say. In asking a question of someone such as, "How was the movie?" or, "How was your vacation?" Listen to hear if the answer sounds superficial. If they say (boringly), "Great, wonderful, couldn't have had a better time," they may be feeling one thing and saying something else. If they sound superficial, probe deeper. Try to listen for emotions. A poor listener listens to facts; a good listener listens to emotions.

*Seventh, a good listener prepares for a conversation.* A psychological framework is needed to orient the listener to a previous conversation. Psychological studies have shown us that memory plays a large part in listening. We are not only able to focus better on a conversation when we remember the previous discussions, but it also helps us to avoid distractions in listening. We are able to focus on the current conversation instead of trying to recall a previous one. A good tip is to have an outline of previous conversations in front of you when you talk. It also gives you a good idea of what further questions to ask and allows you to put information into a logical and flowing framework for ready referral. Still, it is very important to keep eye contact with the speaker. Taking your eyes off the speaker and looking at a page while you take notes is not only discourteous, but you will lose rapport with your prospect. It is very important to jot short notes instead of writing long drawn-out dissertations on the words you hear. Also, it is important to remember that we cannot do two things at once. Psychologically, it is very difficult to engage in more than one activity such as watching TV and also reading the newspaper. Listening to the radio and trying to listen to someone else can result in a loss of comprehension in both. We have a resource pool of attention in our minds that we use in listening. That resource pool is used up by things that we are listening to. Even though we can drive and listen at the same time because we are using two different senses, hearing should involve only one input at a time. When you speak to someone with whom you have had a prior conversation, put the notes in front of you when you talk to that individual again. It will help you stick to the point and make you much more efficient during the discussion. A good listener prepares for a conversation.

*Eighth, a good listener adjusts thought speed to speech speed.* We speak at approximately 200 words per minute. We think four times that fast. Unfortunately, a poor listener just can't adjust. Physiologically, we can't speak as fast as we think. A poor listener tends to drift off and become distracted. He often becomes bored with the conversation that is not moving quickly enough, especially if it isn't on a subject that the listener loves. I spoke to a manager recently who was not very articulate, succinct, or concise in his thinking. I remember him describing his current profit picture for the quarter. He said, "Well, ah, Kerry we are not...looking...um very good...uh this...quarter but, um, I think that ah in the, ah, long run for the ah year, we..should spurt out of this...ah...slump...we are ah having and, uh, well, I think it will look...better for us later." I found myself drifting off while listening to him. I even started daydreaming out of boredom. Not only was he failing to keep my attention, but he wasn't even speaking at 200 words per minute. I was thinking more than four times as fast as he was talking. When you encounter people who speak as slow as this or even when you feel that you are having trouble paying attention, try to anticipate what the speaker is going to say next. If you anticipate the next point and if you guess right, you are way ahead of the game. If you guess wrong, you still have kept yourself attentive enough to listen to hear what he is saying. Mentally summarize what has been said up to that point. Keep a mental bank of the main ideas the speaker has made.

Being a good listener takes work and practice. One great philosopher said, "It is not that we should all be great communicators; it is that we should be less feeble communicators." It is a well known fact that in our highly sophisticated society those of us who listen well tend to make more money and seem to be more successful. Be a good listener. It will help you in business and in your private life. God gave us two ears and only one mouth. Maybe we shouldn't try to outsmart our Maker.

Aside from listening well, there are other methods for increasing sales. We'll discuss one of these, the art of persuasion, next.

# PART 17

# PERSUADING PEOPLE TO BUY

Life would be a lot easier and more productive if the people we interact with saw eye to eye with us all the time. But in reality we must influence these people and persuade them to accept our ideas. *Persuasion* has been defined as that which causes an attitude change through the installation and implementation of ideas. During the course of this chapter we will look at what persuasion is, why it is sometimes difficult to change the attitudes of others, and outline some techniques you may find useful in getting a persuasive message across. The Bible says that Samson slew the Philistines with the jawbone of an ass. Unfortunately the same weapon is still used in business today. The definition of an influential and persuasive salesperson is someone who tells the prospect exactly what he or she wants to hear. Unfortunately, we often don't know what the listener wants to hear. Consequently, we need to know more about how to persuade others, as well as being able to cause others to act on our messages. This can be done in various ways.

Four of the most important elements in the persuasive process are the basic interests and desires that all humans have. These four basic interests and desires are, security, a desire for acceptance, ego satisfaction, and a desire for physical comforts. An understanding and utilization of these four elements will help you become a better persuader. Utilizing these elements when you speak will help you influence people, even if you don't have a golden tongue, a gift of gab or aren't a *natural* salesperson.

## SECURITY

The first element is security. Many salespeople realize that in order to sell a product they must give their prospects a sense of security when dealing with them or give the feeling that they, as salespeople, are concerned with their prospects' well-being. They must develop trust. Frequently, prospects say they are uncomfortable with salespeople. They feel that the salesperson really isn't interested in what they want or need but is merely desirous of making a buck off of the sale. In setting the stage for the persuasive process, security plays a big part. Recently, my secretary bought a new car. She had been to a number of different automobile dealerships and found herself in yet another one. After a short time, she realized that she wasn't going to get any better deal from this dealer than she would from the others, so she started to leave his office. As she walked out, he noticed the tires on the car that she wanted to trade in. He said to her, "Ma'am, I just can't let you leave here with those bad tires. In fact, I can't let you potentially harm yourself or your child by driving home on the freeway with bald tires like that. Those are so dangerous that I would feel personally responsible if something happened. Why don't you leave your car here and drive that new one home today?" That is all my secretary needed to hear to buy the car from this dealer. She felt that he really had concern for her safety. He did get the sale and she went home with the new car.

Another aspect of the security need is the fact that we all want to keep what we have. Most of us will work harder to keep what we have than we will to get something bigger and better. We feel we have worked hard to earn what we have and don't want to lose it. One of the reasons college graduates go for secure jobs in industry is because they feel that they don't want to take a risk, an emotional risk of testing themselves. A salesman friend of mine and I had lunch. All he had was soup. I said, "John, are you on a diet?" He responded, "No, I'm on a commission." Many college graduates believe that if you are on a commission you will be eating soup for a long time. Violating this fundamental desire for security puts a wall up against any persuasive message. Most people will work harder during recessionary periods than they will during boom periods in the country's economy. They get scared and become upset, fearing that they will lose something. Some take on a second job.

In order to develop security, first you must develop rapport. You must cause the person you are persuading to be receptive through building trust and empathy. As with the automobile transaction, the salesman didn't build trust by offering the same deal as every other dealer in town. He got the sale because he showed an interest in her security and well-being.

## ACCEPTANCE

The second element in the persuasion process is acceptance. We all have a deep need to be accepted by others we respect.

From early childhood we struggle to be accepted by our peers. As adolescents, we dressed the same way as our friends. Even as adults, we buy the same toys for our children. We frequently use the same expressions, jargon, and slang as those we see often. During the 1976 Winter Olympics, Dorothy Hamill won a gold medal in women's figure skating. She had an interesting, geometric hair cut that the whole world fell in love with. Just a few short months after winning the medal, thousands and thousands of other women around the world were wearing the *Dorothy Hamill* haircut.

In Paris and New York, where the fashion elite decides what the rest of the world will wear, style is set by designers. When long hems were popular, a few celebrities wore them immediately. More and more followed. The reason fashions catch on so quickly is that when a few respected people wear them, others want to identify and be part of the "in group."

Years ago, metal tennis racquets were the rage. Within a few short months of their debut, almost every tennis player had one. In many ways, the racquets were inferior to the sturdy wood ones.

This desire to be accepted by other people is a true universal trait. An example of this acceptance phenomenon is George Carlin. A friend of mine recently met George in an airport in Atlanta, Georgia. After speaking to him for a few minutes, he asked Carlin, "How did you ever get to be a comedian?" Carlin answered, "That is simple to answer; I merely started out trying to be funny because of a deep desire for people to like me. I wanted people to enjoy being around me. In fact, Carlin told my friend that many comedians start out that same way. They want to be accepted by others. Out of a sense of emotional insecurity, they want people to love them. A desire for acceptance can be applied in the persuasive process by using a compliment or an expression of liking. Joe Girard, a self-made millionaire who sells more cars and trucks, than anybody in the world, originated what he calls *the law of 250*. Girard believes that every customer comes in contact with at least 250 people every month. He believes that each person he sells a car to will tell at least 250 people what they think of their car and Joe Girard. In turn, they will keep on referring other people to him. He will soon have a huge group of prospects from that one sale. Joe Girard goes a step further and appeals to the customer's desires, for acceptance. Whenever he sells a car to someone, he finds out their birthday and wedding anniversary. After the sale is consummated, he sends them a card saying, "Thanks for buying your car from Joe Girard. I like you." The "I like you" represents an appeal to the customer's need for acceptance from Joe Girard. He also sends cards whenever the customer has a birthday and a wedding anniversary. This play on acceptance in persuasion works so well that Joe Girard has the highest repeat sales and rate of referrals of anybody in the industry. It is hard to believe that anyone who bought a car from Joe, even if the car ended up having problems, wouldn't go back to Joe Girard again. Joe showed them that he liked them and projected acceptance. The prospect thinks of him as "good ole" Joe Girard instead of, "the guy I bought my car from."

Joe Gondolpho, a salesman from Florida who sells more life insurance than anyone else in the country, also has a method of projecting acceptance. Joe prospects a number of different career groups. Among his prospects are blue-collar miners. He drives up to the mine, meets the miners, and tries to establish rapport. He realizes that they would be "put offish" and "suspect" of him if he dressed in a normal suit. In the trunk of his car, Joe has an old dirty shirt and a pair of pants that have seen better days. He rolls up the sleeves on his shirt, puts on his old pants, and also wears a hard hat. His hit ratio is very high. He tries to be one of the men; he wants to be accepted on equal terms by his appearance.

## EGO SATISFACTION

Third, we all have an interest and desire for ego satisfaction.

We spend our lifetimes developing our egos. We want to preserve them. We want to maintain a positive self-image. Anything that may potentially deflate or damage that hard-earned ego will meet with great defensiveness and resistance. There are many things that cause us to be defensive and have a lack of receptivity. Among those is the theory of the 100 abuses. The theory says that we are emotionally abused daily. We each have at least 100 things happen to us every day which hurt our self-image and abuse our egos. Have you ever been put on hold on the telephone for ten minutes? Have you ever been cut off on the freeway or had someone hang up the phone on you? Have you ever done something nice for someone who was ungrateful? This happens to each and every one of us every day. It causes us to be defensive and resistant to new ideas because the unknown could potentially hurt our egos

One example of the role that egos play in our lives is seen in the bragging that people do. I think almost all of us have from time to time bragged about a great feat or something we think is impressive. When we buy a new car, we frequently say, "See that little red car over there. I bought that for $2,999. Not only am I a good negotiator, but I really know what I am doing." What is being communicated here? Psychologically, we are saying, "Look at me. I am here. I am important." I recently went to a men's clothing store looking for a new suit. I tried on the jacket and pants. The salesman walked over and said, "How do you like it?" I replied, "Well, it's nice but how much is it?" After he told me I said, "I don't want to buy the store, I just want this suit." Then he asked me what I did for a living. I told the salesman that I was a professional speaker and that I traveled around the country speaking at seminars and conferences. The salesman said, "Sir, a man as important and prestigious as you needs to look as good as he possibly can. I think this suit makes you look like the important person that you obviously are." Well, that's all it took. I asked the price one more time and said, "Where do I sign?" We all know the Golden Rule: Do unto others as you would have them do unto you. But I prefer to rephrase, Do unto me as I would have done unto myself. Treat me like I want to be treated. I don't want to be abused. My ego wants to be preserved.

Recently, while I was consulting for a computer corporation, I spoke to a personnel firm who was placing a man in our organization. When I called a manager of the firm on the phone, he had an interesting way of boosting my ego. He said "Dr. Johnson, it's great to talk to you." Then he said, "Jenny, hold all my calls. Kerry is on the phone." If the conversation was two minutes or twenty, he would always end with, "Kerry, it has been a pleasure talking to you. Please call any time." Even though this may sound phony to you, I always went away from a conversation with that man feeling warm and good about myself. Because of this appeal to my ego, we did a lot of business with his firm.

## PHYSICAL COMFORTS

The fourth of the primary interests and desires is for physical comforts. Madison Avenue advertising firms in New York City deal in persuasion on a mass scale. They try to promote happy lives through buying their products. Their persuasive message is, "We know how to solve your problems; buy our products." People buy products or services to satisfy their perceived needs. A good example of this is a Japanese car commercial. A millionaire is being chauffeured in his small import to a mansion. When he gets to his estate, the chauffeur opens the door for him and asks, "What will you do with all the money you saved from buying this car?" The millionaire looks at the chauffeur saying, "I believe I'll save that, too." It makes the viewer think that if he, too, buys Japanese sports cars, he'll save a lot of money and become a millionaire. The lesson here is to always realize that the person you are speaking to has a deep and emotional desire for physical comforts. He will try anything within reason to try to make life happier through the acquisition of material things in an attempt to become more fulfilled in life.

By being aware of these four universal human interests and desires, security, acceptance, ego satisfaction, and physical comforts, and by appealing to your prospect's desire for these needs, the persuasion process will become a very easy and pleasant experience without coercion or forced decisions.

## RECEPTIVENESS

In the persuasion process, we must always be aware of the important role that receptivity plays. Your listener must be receptive to your message if he is to accept it. Receptivity is defined as being open and responsive to ideas and suggestions while being willing and ready to accept them. One of the major roadblocks to receptivity is distraction. The people we persuade must not be distracted either from inner or outer, internal or external preoccupations or influences. As a consultant for a major firm, I was given the task of evaluating employee productivity. After a few weeks of researching and interviewing employees, I formed a recommendation that I wanted one manager to implement. This manager had a corner office which was enclosed by glass on two sides. I made an appointment about one o'clock to speak to him about my ideas. The secretaries in the building were just coming back from lunch. After a few short minutes it became apparent to me that it was going to be difficult to speak to him because of his distraction of looking out the window at the secretaries. Another common setting in which people may become very distracted is in a restaurant. One person has only a blank wall or the kitchen to focus on while the other has clear view of everyone who enters and exits. Be sure to sit your client in the seat facing the wall or kitchen. You will be able to insure a much higher level of receptivity than if he is allowed to watch all the activity in the restaurant.

Another problem in establishing receptivity is the distance between a present attitude and the new idea you may be trying to get the person to adopt. It is much easier to try to get an arch conservative, hard-line Republican to become a liberal Democrat than it is to get a secretary to move her lunch to 12 o'clock from one o'clock. Although this seems difficult, in some instances when there is a great distance between two attitudes, it is not impossible. One of the important facets of establishing receptivity is the effect that a new idea or attitude change may have on the person's ego and self-image. As was outlined before, ego plays a great part in attitude change. Twenty years ago, when computer firms were vigorously marketing business computers, many business people felt that they did not need a computer because they had no problems with their information systems. Some felt the company productivity possibly could be improved upon, but it was something that internal management could deal with. Consequently, many computer firms had trouble marketing the early computers because of management egos and overconfidence. It is important to realize ego position in any persuasive message. One of the toughest things to get through in penetrating a wall, or attitude barrier, is the ego.

## THE PERSUASIVE PROCESS

Let's look at the persuasive process technically. Questions and expressions of doubt usually indicate receptivity. Flat statements, such as "that price is too high," indicate low receptivity or rejection as opposed to an open question, such as "why should I pay your price when I can get it for 10 percent less elsewhere?" Receptivity also increases with the degree of questioning. The question, why should I pay your price, is much less receptive than how much is it? When a prospect makes a flat assertion in opposition to an idea, you must be careful not to cause that individual to be more defensive by allowing the conversation to lead to an argument, but instead use a technique to cause the individual to be more receptive. Respect that individual's stand on a subject in order to try to persuade him; explore that person's position, and try to find a weakness in his argument. Lead that person through an objective survey of his position. In doing this, one of two things will be found: you will find that the argument is sound, in which case it is probably a good idea to drop your attempt at a persuasive message. Or, on the other hand, you will be able to find a weak point in the argument. This weakness serves as an opening and as a place to insert your persuasive message. Also, when a roadblock is encountered, it is important to remember that in order to keep the individual from becoming defensive, you must withhold your argument until the other person becomes more receptive. Years ago the Los Angeles Dodgers played the New York Yankees. A player on the Yankee team was called out trying to steal second base. Manager Billy Martin tried to persuade the umpire he was wrong; the umpire crossed his arms in a defensive position and looked up at the sky. After a few moments, Billy Martin went back to his seat and sat down. Martin waited for the umpire to drop his arms and then walked back on the field to argue again. Frequently, we see examples of this in people we try to persuade. Even though they may not look up at the sky and cross their arms, they are giving us the same blank stare. We feel as though we are speaking to a brick wall.

A real estate manager is trying to convince an agent to spend more time prospecting on the telephone, farming, and spend less time taking floor time, waiting for the phone to ring. The manager said, "What do you think? Do you feel that you should spend more time prospecting?" The agent answered, "I could make better use of my time picking up requests and following up on them. I don't think it is good utilization of time asking for listings door to door. I may not get more people, but the prospects I get from floor time in the long run will be much more beneficial." The weakness in this argument is the agent saying, "I may not get more prospects." The manager looked at that as his opening and he inserted his message, "You need more prospects, I agree. Prospecting will give you that. You can continue to have floor time too, but you will have more people to work with if you prospect well."

In a persuasive message, the same technique can be used in persuading someone to make an attitude change or to implement one of your ideas. Another important point to remember is to present your ideas and promptly get feedback. Psychological studies have shown us that we shouldn't speak to anyone for more than thirty seconds without getting their response. After twenty seconds there is too much information for most people to absorb and remember. Get response and feedback as to how that person feels about your message.

I taught a class at the University of California on introductory psychology. About midway through the class, one man raised his hand and said, "I'm confused." I asked at what point he got confused. He retorted, "After you said, 'good morning class.'" Be sure you ask for feedback. It instills acceptance as well as preserves the ego – ("your opinions, Mr. Prospect, are important").

## THE COMMANDER SYNDRONE

Another important point to remember in persuasion is called the *commander syndrome*. The more a person is governed by the need to prove himself, the less likely he is to be receptive to another person's logic. The commander syndrome dictates that various people need to persuade themselves in accepting ideas, not you. They may not be easily persuaded. Ideas must be made to seem to come from the person they are addressed to. An example of this was the popular show, *Mash*. On that show,

Colonel Blake frequently thought out loud while he believed Radar would help him with his thoughts. In one episode, Radar came to Colonel Blake and said, "Sir, we are almost out of medical supplies." Colonel Blake said, "What? We're out of supplies?" Radar had a quick solution: "Let's call up the 4076th and see if they can give us some supplies until we get more from Tokyo." Colonel Blake said, "I've got it! Radar, go over to the 4076th and ask if we can have some medical supplies until we can get more from Toyko." Even though it was first presented by Radar, the idea was again presented by Colonel Blake as though it was his original idea.

This need is frequently found in people who have fairly low self-esteem and a need to take credit themselves. In situations such as this, try to give the listeners the impression that you are a neutral information broker. Let them pick which avenue to take. Give them a number of different suggestions and alternatives, such as, "Colonel Blake, we could order some supplies from Tokyo which may take two weeks, get interim supplies from the 4076th, or we can shut down part of our hospital due to lack of supplies." It becomes obvious in this case that borrowing the supplies is the best solution. But giving a choice to an individual will help this person feel as though the decision was all his. He will be much happier with that decision, with the added advantage of preserving his ego. If the individual picks the wrong avenue, or if he becomes negative, offer additional information and ask him to re-evaluate. By all means do not try to convince this individual that your way is the only right one.

The theory of free-floating receptivity is one that will usually prevent any roadblocks or defensiveness from coming up. This law of free-floating receptivity dictates that the more positive people feel towards you, the more receptive they will be toward your suggestions. This is a valuable application for anyone. It dictates that if people feel positive and good about you, they will be very receptive toward you. As a result it will be much easier to persuade them.

A working knowledge of persuasion techniques will help you become a better communicator and get your message across. Persuasive people are often described as successful or winners. They typically are impressive people who command high salaries because they are able to get a message across, make it believable, and are accepted by other people. Persuasion is a learned set of techniques. We are not born with it. Use these ideas to get others to accept your message. You'll be surprised at how well they work.

Putting your techniques of persuasion to work requires prospects. One means of acquiring new prospects, the referral system, is discussed in the next chapter.

# PART 18

## HOW TO USE
### REFERRALS

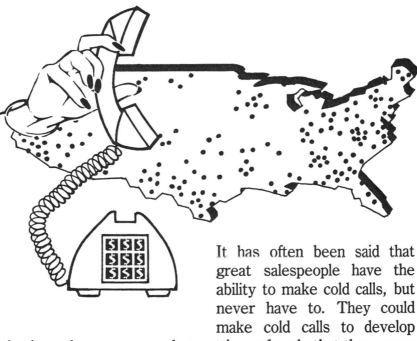

It has often been said that great salespeople have the ability to make cold calls, but never have to. They could make cold calls to develop business but are so good at getting referrals that they never need to put themselves through the high stress and rejection. This next chapter is not only on getting referrals, but using those referrals to produce more business. You will learn to use referrals to produce more business than you have had before. The best way of increasing your sales production and decrease business development time is by using the networks that already exist between your existing clients and your new prospects.

It's Carl's sixteenth cold call, and he's had fifteen rejections in a row. "There must be a better way," he says to himself.

"I might as well be calling right out of the telephone book." As he dials, his secret hope is that he'll get either a busy signal or no answer. He wonders if there's a job that doesn't create so much emotional distress. There has to be a better way!

If you're still making cold calls to get business, you undoubtedly don't enjoy it. In fact, you probably dread any phone time that is forced on you. There is a better way. Learn how to use referrals. You've probably heard these often-used excuses for not getting referrals: "If my client really wanted to give me a referral, he would have offered it" or, "If my work was really outstanding, I would have too many referrals." How about this reluctant thought: "When it gets down to the point of asking for a referral, I lose my nerve. I just don't feel comfortable asking my clients for leads." The truth of the matter is that your clients think you are already extremely successful. That is the image you project in marketing. As a client once said, "I was shocked when my accountant asked me for a referral. I never before realized they made a difference in his business."

Many salespeople use effective referral-generating techniques. Some, like Dennis Renter, a Newport Beach, California financial planner, hands out cards to clients offering free introductory appointments. He encourages clients to hand them out to friends who might benefit from his services.

## REFERRAL TIPS

The best referral technique comes from Ron Howard in Los Gatos, California, a salesperson with a real estate syndication company. Ron is an ex-financial planner who moved from Salt Lake City, Utah to San Jose, California, where he had no clients, no prospects, and no referrals. His "mind-set philosophy" conveys a message parallel to, "Give a man a fish and he will eat for a day; teach a man to fish and he will eat for a lifetime." His attitude dictates, "If I make a sale, I eat for a day; if I get referrals, I will eat for a lifetime."

Ron's technique focuses on asking for referrals during the closing process. His closes center on both assumptive and alternate-of-choice techniques. A favorite approach is, "How much money would you like to invest?" He also uses the simple question, "What program do you like the best?" At the point the prospect says yes, Ron takes an application from his briefcase and explains that he needs some information. He admitted to me that he usually has enough details already to fill out the application, but the request sets the stage for gaining referrals. When he's working with a married couple, he usually asks the husband to answer selective details, and then gives the wife a piece of paper and a pen. He asks, "Would you please fill this out, listing four or five people you know who have common sense, can save some money, and may wish to invest." Ron then turns back to the husband and completes the details.

## WHO TO REFER

Ron has often been interrupted by the spouse asking, "Exactly who do I put down?" He replies, "Just four or five people you know socially or professionally with good common sense, can save money, and may wish to invest." Ron usually receives three or four names. His closing average of 80 percent - 85 percent on referrals is probably due to prompting of even the most reluctant clients for referrals. He softens his close by explaining how he will deal with the names. For instance, Ron may state, "I want to meet with people like yourselves so that I can share some investment ideas. I will respect the fact that you are friends and there won't be any high pressure. I will strive to help them in much the same way as I have helped you." Obviously, if you don't sell investment products, this strategy will apply to cars, stocks, or tomatoes. You still need to use your existing customers and clients for referrals.

## FIVE STEPS TO GAIN REFERRALS

Some general rules in asking for referrals are: 1) Tell your clients why you need them. 2) Mention that you will respect their relationship with the referral, as well as the referring client's financial privacy. 3) Be specific. Instead of requesting "a few names," ask for five referrals. You are much more likely to get what you ask for when you give an exact number. 4) Learn something about each referral's personal life. Does she play tennis? Is his hobby, interior design? You will be able to develop a high level of trust and rapport by initially saying, "Jan tells me you're quite a racquetball player." Using personal knowledge like this will also position you as a friend of a friend. It will make it very difficult for a prospect to say no to an appointment request. 5) Get the referral before the paper work is done. Have you noticed how quickly busy clients want to get back to their office or home after business has been completed. If they sense that giving you referrals is part of the sales process, they'll give you more qualified names.

I recently received a referral to an insurance company executive who was in charge of booking speakers for his annual convention. The executive was described as an avid hockey fan who coached his son's hockey team. I called and told him who had referred me to him. He was fairly guarded on the telephone until I said, "Mr. White, I hear you're a hockey coach." He responded with enthusiasm, "Yes, I am." I explained that my son, Neil, had been playing hockey for about three years, and was having trouble getting "checked" by his opponents. We spoke about hockey for a few minutes. Fifteen minutes later, he booked me for his company's convention. I may have gained the business engagement without using this personal touch, but five minutes of personal conversation about a mutual interest helped develop trust more rapidly than two weeks of face-to-face meetings. Using these five steps will help you get at least eight appointments for every ten referrals.

## HIGH VISIBILITY

A great salesperson is extremely effective at cold calling but never has to take that route. Instead, use the referral-generating technique of keeping yourself memorable in your client's mind. Joe Gerard, the *Guinness Book of World Records,* "Best Salesman on Earth," reports that everyone has at least 250 friends and acquaintances who are contacted at least once each month. Obviously, your client is able to give more than five referrals! Ron Howard uses another effective device for gathering referrals. He asks his clients to hand him their personal telephone book. Ron then turns the book to "H" and writes in "Ron Howard" and his telephone number. He also turns to "F" for Financial services and writes in the name of his company, Investors Financial Planning, with his name and phone number underneath. Ron reports that the average client will refer another twenty to thirty of his friends and acquaintances using this method. He has even been called from cocktail parties by clients who want him to schedule an appointment with their "good buddy" (they just met).

## CREATING OPPORTUNITIES

Often salespeople have difficulty conducting a yearly review with existing clients. But think what you could gain by providing that service. You guessed it — five new solid referrals. Ask the question of your clients, "Do you know anybody I should meet?" Then move again into your qualification statement: "I would like the names of any social or professional people you know who can save money, have good common sense and might wish to invest."

## THE FINAL SCENARIO

As Carl dialed the telephone, he kept thinking about his client. The client told Carl that the referral was an avid golfer. Carl himself was just learning the game. The referral owned his own business and was a progressive thinker and investor. Carl made the call. He mentioned his client's name. The referral answered, "Yes, he told me you would be calling. I've been looking forward to talking with you." Carl smiled.

## REFERRAL SCRIPT

The following is a script you may find useful in following up with your new referrals. Use this as a foundation, then work your own style into the model. Let it serve simply as a guideline, not to be read, but rather to be conceptually followed.

## *INTRODUCTION*

Hello. Is this Mr. Jones? (referral name) My name is (your name). I am with (company name). I spent some time with a mutual friend recently (client's first and last name). Do you remember him?

## *RAPPORT GENERATION*

He tells me you (personal touch — background, hobby) are a great tennis player. Is that true? (Allow enough time to elicit rapport).

## APPOINTMENT PRESENTATION

I've had the opportunity to share an interesting and inventive idea with (client's name) that he found very exciting. In fact, he was so interested that he incorporated it into his own investment plan. He gave me your name and thought you might be interested also. Of course, I have no way of knowing if it would be of benefit to you, but (clients' name) did recommend that I call you to set up a time when we could talk and share a few ideas. Did (clients' name) tell you I would be calling? (Yes, No) How about Tuesday at 3 p.m. or is 4:30 p.m. best for you?

## APPOINTMENT CLOSE

Do you have thirty minutes later this week when we could get together. Or (for appointment close): I'll be in your neighborhood Wednesday at about 4 p.m. Are you free then?

Referrals are not like good wine and cheddar cheese. They do not improve with age. CALL REFERRALS WITHIN 48 HOURS. The first person to ask about your progress with referrals will be your client. If he knows you pursued his lead, he is likely to give you other names. If he thinks otherwise, gaining more referrals from him will be tougher than arm-wrestling a grizzly. Also, remember to copy your first letter of correspondence to the client who gave you the referral. He may help sell you with a telephone call.

It's so important to get your referral involved in prospecting. You may in fact gain 25 percent more business, just by virtue of letting your referral know that you've actually contacted the leads he gave you. I recently prospected a president of one of the largest investment broker/dealer corporations in America. One individual, Sam Bartholomew, heard me speak and gave me the name of the president of a company called Integrated Resources. I called this gentleman and mentioned my referral's name, Sam Bartholomew. I said, "Mr. Krat, Sam Bartholomew mentioned your name and thought you might be able to use a speaker at your next sales conference." We went on with the conversation and he requested that I send him information. I sincerely believed that he was ready to hire me because I qualified him; he had the money, the need, and a date for me to speak. I not only copied a letter to Sam Bartholomew, but also called Sam and thanked him for the referral. That same day Sam called Mr. Krat and told him that I would be excellent for the program and that he should hire me as soon as possible to speak to his representatives. Mr. Krat called me back the next week and booked me for five programs. Yes, you can get referrals involved in selling for you if you let them know you are following up. The added benefit is that if your referral feels that you have actually taken the leads he has given you and followed up, he will give you more leads.

I have another friend in Vancouver, British Columbia, named Murray Nielson. Murray, at one point, was the program chairman for the association of life insurance salespeople called the Life Underwriters. When Murray used me to speak, he gave me the names of five people whom I should contact around Canada. Not only did I call those people, but I sent Murray the copies of the letters I sent to these individuals and thanked him personally for the referrals he gave me. I even gave him a present of a watch that I purchased in Hong Kong the year before. That was three years ago. To this day Murray is still sending me referrals. He once told me that he enjoys giving me referrals so much that practically everyone he talks to may have a need for a consultant/speaker like me. He prospects them for me. Your clients will be your best source of business. All you need to do is ask them to refer you. But more importantly, let them know that you didn't just take the leads and throw them in your briefcase. Your clients want to see you become successful. They want to see you become wealthy. Let them know that you are appreciative and that you have followed up on the leads they gave you. They will give you many more in the months and years to come.

Even the best of referrals need to be won over initially. In the next chapter we will examine ways of overcoming objections.

# PART 19

# OVERCOMING ANY OBJECTION

Ned was feeling confident! After meeting twice with his prospective client, Ned knew he had the perfect product. He had invested a great deal of time in this case. It could be the biggest single commission of his year. Ned even mentally told himself that his personal reward for closing the deal would be a trip to Hawaii with his family.

He planned the presentation and close with the precision of a tactical S.W.A.T. team. Ned knew exactly how to convince his prospect that the product benefits were unequaled. No other program could perform as well. But. . . . his prospect said, "It's too expensive. It's too complex. My associates will never buy it. We're evaluating another company. We'll get back to you."

Ned believed he was a good closer, yet he never got the chance to practice his skills. His prospect gave objection after objection. Could the information he'd gained through probing have been that far off? Every time he answered one objection, his prospect came up with another. Ned knew his stuff. He had been selling for a decade. What could or should he have done?

Your prospects won't buy until they trust you! Prospects don't trust products, they trust people. Even though your prospect trusts you, he may give you objections. This chapter, overcoming and cashing in on objections, will give you very specific and useful techniques on turning any objection or resistance into a request for information that you can satisfy and thereby close. You will learn techniques on turning your prospect's uneasiness into trust that you will then use to help them buy from you.

## DEVELOP RAPPORT

Why do prospects give objections? There are a myriad of reasons, some of which have nothing to do with the product or service. But they all have to do with your level of rapport. If you believe that trust comes from rapport, then you must believe that rapport comes from being similar to the prospect. Similarity comes from finding a common ground with your prospect and letting him know you have listened, understood, and cared about his problems.

Another speaker uses the analogy between marriage and objections when he asks his audience which emotion is the opposite of love. He reports that unmarried people often state that hate is the antithesis of love. The response from those who are married is that indifference is its deadly opposite. His conclusion is that as long as there is strong positive or negative emotion in a marriage, both partners care. But if either partner shows indifference, all is lost. When indifference takes over, whether in sales or marriage, the common ground is permanently gone. Neither one cares enough to try to work things out. Sales works the same way. As long as your prospect gives you resistance in an objection, you know he cares. But if he tries to ignore you or says, "I'm not interested," get ready to call your next prospect. If you get an objection, consider yourself fortunate. Your prospect cares and is requesting more information. Sometimes though, you may mistakenly shoot yourself in the foot and push your prospect into giving you an objection.

While at a conference, I was approached by a wholesaler, so engrossed with his product that he thought it would sell itself. His only attempt at developing rapport with me was to ask if I would like a 30 percent annual return on my money. Then, without waiting for my answer, he launched into a four minute monologue. He was startled when I interrupted him to say, "I have no idea what you're talking about."

You're sure to get an objection if you talk for more than thirty seconds at a time. If you talk for a longer period, you're bound to lose rapport. Television commercials are thirty seconds in duration for a very important reason. Television viewers stop watching after thirty seconds. It's a waste of advertising dollars. The average length of a camera shot is 4.5 seconds. Hollywood is well aware of the human attention span.

## THE PERFECT SALE

There are pragmatic reasons why you receive objections. First, you haven't thoroughly probed your prospect's needs. The four stages of a perfect sale are: approach, probe, present, and close. The probe is the primary stage. If you find out what your prospect needs, and also what he wants, he will buy from you. Rarely will you receive insurmountable objections from a prospect when you have listened effectively. Few salespeople listen to their prospects. They think that since they've heard the problem before, they already know the answer.

There is a difference between a peddler and a salesperson. A peddler is an individual who tries to convince anyone he possibly can to purchase his product. But a professional salesperson, tries to solve problems. He tries to match his product or service to his prospect's needs. He also tries to find out their goals and objectives and literally attempts to take problems off their worry list. This means that he is a problem solver who makes money by prescribing solutions rather than hawking his wares.

I recently bought an insurance policy from a salesperson I thought was excellent. Not only did he find out my needs by asking various, specific questions to determine my goals, but he also spent the balance of the first interview solely asking questions to find solutions. The second time I saw him, he presented ideas I thought were useful in solving some of my problems. Another salesperson I met, the total opposite of the fine problem-solving colleague, listened to me talk for about four minutes and immediately told me what I needed. While they both probed, one actually tried to get inside my head to find out what I needed in a product, and also knew how I wanted to be treated emotionally.

Second, the risk/reward ratio is too close. Your prospect will give you objections if he feels that the risk of loss is close to or greater than the rewarding benefits of your product. Often that risk is an expenditure of money or time. The reward should clearly appeal to your prospect's own ideas of reward, not yours. This comes from knowing what your prospect wants and making sure they are satisfied.

Have you ever bought a product where the amount of money required to buy it made you so uncomfortable that the benefits didn't overcome the discomfort? A few years ago, I bought a limited partnership in an almond orchard. Before the new tax legislation, almonds were showing 7 to 8 percent cash flow profit per year with about a 35 percent tax write-off. The amount of money required to buy into the almond orchard was about $10,000, paid over a three-year period. Unfortunately, there were many investments I had to choose from. Since inflation at the time was right around 6 percent, I felt that I wasn't getting enough benefit to justify such a large expenditure. I realized that outside of the tax benefits, I only gained about 1 or 2 percent after inflation. The reward of making a very high expenditure, in my opinion, was not worth the risk taken.

Third, the prospect fears making quick decisions. While most states allow a three-day "no regret period" in which a decision may be reversed, a hesitant prospect might simply say, "I just want to think about it." What he's actually telling you is, "Things are moving too quickly for me. I don't want to make a fast decision. I need more time."

Do you remember your last big purchase, such as a house or a car? At one time, even within the last year, you may have felt buyer's remorse. Buyer's remorse is a significant factor in the purchase of any product. The basic reason you may feel this is that you may not think your judgment is well developed enough to make a large-purchase decision. You have misgivings and feel that you didn't have all the information that you needed to make a proper decision. For that reason alone, most of us feel that making a buying decision will probably be disastrous. Last year I bought several computers for my office. These computer systems seemed appropriate, since they included very good word processing software for my staff. The expense of buying this equipment was enormously high, one of the biggest purchases I have made for my business. But my computer system is crucial to the level of efficiency and administrative effectiveness in my office. While the salesman was trying to close me on buying the computers, I found myself procrastinating a decision. I said to him, "Gee, I think I'd like to wait and think about it for a while." My wife, Sandy, was with me that day. She said, "Kerry, we need these. Why not just get them now?" While I realized that she was absolutely right, I still felt trepidation in rushing into the purchase too quickly. Fortunately, as is often the case in my business, the purchases I decided to make were the right ones.

Fourth, your prospect is not convinced that your solution will work. I'm sure you've heard this before, "That's what you say," or, "Sounds good, but will it work?" Your prospect is begging you for proof. He is saying, "If you can back up your claims with facts, I'll buy."

There are three things your prospect consistently thinks whenever you present a solution: 1) Prove it to me. 2) Prove it to me. 3) Prove it to me. Your prospect wants you to prove things that he may be skeptical of. More importantly, he wants proof of those things that he has not had experience with before. I recently talked with an attendee at one of my presentations who wanted to buy a program entitled, "The Psychology of Productivity." I explained the benefits of the program and stated that if he used the six tape audio cassette programs, it would increase his sales by 70 percent within six weeks. He lowered his glasses to the bridge of his nose and looked over the top of them at me. I could tell right away that he was not sure that my recommended program would work. But when I gave him examples of people who had used the approach and what they achieved, his trepidation turned into acceptance. He grew more enthusiastic and bought my tape package. Fortunately I proved the product benefits before he produced an objection. I was able to avoid his resistance. Had I not been able to read his skepticism, I would not have been able to make that sale as quickly as I did.

Fifth, he was told to raise an objection. Whether you know it or not, many of your prospects came to you pre-armed with objections, no matter how much they like the product. Their Uncle Howard said, "Don't let those guys rip you off on that investment like they did me," or, "Don't buy anything except term insurance. Otherwise the insurance company gives you cash values far lower than any investment you could have."

## EIGHT-STEP FORMULA

There is a way to cash in an objection, no matter what the reason. This eight step formula will help eliminate at least 50 percent of the objections that you come up against in your career.

1) *Hear them out.* Most salespeople think they already know what the prospect will say before he says it. A prospect of mine, is a vice president in a real estate syndication company. I had previously spoken to an associate of his about using me as a sales speaker at one of his product seminars. When I asked him if he was still interested in my participation, he said, "Well, your speaking fee is really too high. I'm not sure I can justify it to my boss." I felt like giving him my favorite price/cost counter with, "When you pay peanuts, you get monkeys." But instead I bit my tongue and waited until he was through talking. To my surprise, he talked himself out of the objection. He said, "You're really too expensive for us. But then again, if you weren't good, I wouldn't want you. I wouldn't expect you to be cheap. If you can generate higher broker attendance at these meetings by presenting effective sales skills, it'll be worth it. Okay, let's do it." He actually answered his own objection. If I had interrupted him, I would have bought the product back.

2) *Cushion it.* You will make more points with your prospect if he realizes that you fully understand his objections and point of view. Practice a technique called *pacing*. Rather than directly answering the objection, repeat it back to your prospect using the same words he used when mentioning it. "Mr Prospect, I understand that seems a little too risky now," or, "Sam, I realize it seems a little too long to hold the investment." When he knows you fully understand what he said, he'll listen much more intently to your answer.

3) *Isolate it.* If you haven't faced a prospect who has given you an objection shopping list yet, you will. Blocking occurs when you simply answer his words without responding to his emotional concerns. For example, "Sam, it's not in my budget now!" or, "Well, I understand how it can fit in my budget, but my CPA has advised me against this type of product," or, "Yes, but I've heard companies like this are not paying off." To

overcome any laundry list of objections he may have, say this, "Mr. Prospect, before I give you an answer, are there any other concerns you have that would prevent you from going ahead with this?" Another way to phrase this is to say, "Are there any other reasons preventing you from moving ahead with this package?" If he says, "Yes, my wife won't let me buy this," you have a real objection. This technique is an effective way to get to the heart of the concern.

4) *Question it.* Never, never, never answer an objection immediately after it is given. Twenty percent of the objections you hear are concerns based on insecurity. The prospect may not think it's important, but he asked it anyway. Allow him the chance to hear his own logic. A prospect once said, "I don't use outside speakers at my conferences because of the expense." I thought he was referring to the speaking fee. But when I asked, "What bothers you specifically about the expense?" he answered, "It's not the fee, it's the travel expenses." "Well, Mr. Prospect, I'll be in your area that week anyway, so travel expenses will only be about $200. How does that sound?" Ask him to first explain what his objections really mean.

5) *Confirm criteria.* This technique is excellent for establishing recommitment. Ms. Prospect may state, "It's too expensive." Your confirming criteria response would be, "Well, I understand you think it's too expensive. If I could show you, instead, that you can afford it, would you go ahead with the purchase?" If she says, "Yes," you have requalified her intent to buy. If she says, "No," there's a much bigger objection behind the one she just gave you. Another way of confirming criteria is to refer back to the goals you discovered during the probing phase. "I understand you believe it's too expensive. However, you told me earlier you wanted a low deductible cost of living allowance and only a three-month waiting period. Is that correct?" Before you answer the objection, first make sure you know what is important to your prospect.

6) *Answer creatively.* Avoid repeating information you've

already given, or at least rephrase it. When you answer creatively, you show your prospect how to solve the problem. For example, the prospect comes to you with a worry list. When you help relieve your prospect's burdens, you get more than just a product order. You gain a life-long referring client. One of the answers to "it costs too much" is, "Ms. Prospect, which is your greatest concern, the price or the cost?" The prospect may reply, "What's the difference between the two?" Explain that the price is the immediate outlay of cash, but the cost is the immediate expenditure compared to the value you receive in return. In other words, "If this product performs the way I have indicated, would the value you receive be worth the price?" This prevents your prospect from having price myopia.

7) *Confirm the answer.* Make sure that you have answered the objection to your prospect's satisfaction. Confirming the answer maintains trust, and also presents an opportunity for you to close. You may say, "Ms. Prospect, does that alleviate your concern about the price?" or, "Did I answer that to your satisfaction?" Every good speaker knows that after he answers a question from an audience member, he must ask the attendee if his question was answered properly. If not, the attendee repeats the question, and the speaker responds again. This confirmation reassures your prospect, in her own mind, that it is no longer a concern.

8) *Close.* This is the easy part. If you've utilized these seven steps is cashing in an objection, your prospect will be ready for you to follow through with the close. Three tried-and-true closes are: the Implied Consent or Assumptive Close, Alternate of Choice, and the "I Recommend" close. I'll discuss more about "closes" in the next chapter.

## PUT IT ALL TOGETHER

Okay, let's put it all together. Each step will fit naturally after you have practiced just a bit. Here's an example of the steps in logical order:

## HEAR HIM OUT

*Prospect*: Don, I'd like to think about this and get back to you later. *Salesperson*: Sure, but why? *Prospect*: Well, the premiums are just out of sight. I don't think it'll work for me right now.

## CUSHION IT, ISOLATE IT

*Salesperson*: I understand that the premiums seem out of sight. Is this your only concern, or is there something else that is preventing you from going ahead with this? *Prospect*: No, it's just that the premiums are too high.

## QUESTION IT

*Salesperson*: Why is this a concern for you? *Prospect*: Well, I spoke to another agent last week who had basically the same plan, but it didn't cost as much.

## CONFIRM CRITERIA

*Salesperson*: Well, Don, you said initially that you wanted protection in case of a disability until age sixty-five with a three-month waiting period, right? You also want business overhead protection. Is that correct? *Prospect*: Yes, that's right.

## ANSWER IT

*Salesperson*: Did the other plan include these aspects with the same product benefits? *Prospect*: No.

## CONFIRM ANSWER

*Salesperson*: That's actually where the higher rate comes in. I understand that these things are important to you. Did I answer that concern of yours about premiums? *Prospect*: Yes.

## CLOSE

*Salesperson*: I think you remember the chart showing the

probability of your having a disabling event before you are forty years old. That's why, with your age bracket, overhead, and personal income, I recommend.................... *Prospect:* Great. It's worth the money. I'll do it!

## OBJECTIONS BECOME OPPORTUNITIES

Don't let your prospect give you a laundry list of objections you shouldn't have to handle. Stay in control. Make sure that what you say is short and sweet. Cash in on objections. They are the tools high producers use to create satisfied clients. Remember, objections are simply opportunities in disguise. Unmask them, and you and your prospect will come away winners.

The final chapter of this section covers closing the sale. Knowing how and when to close is as important as the techniques of getting a prospect to buy discussed in the preceding chapters.

# PART 20

---

# CLOSING TECHNIQUES OF THE BIG HITTERS

Are you good at closing a sale? If you're like most sales pros, you're not only knowledgeable about how to close but also realize that without the ability to close, you also will lose your source of income. But closing is not the most important part of the sale, probing is. If you can probe well and discover your prospect's real needs, you will close with few objections. If you don't probe well, you'll be beset with objections that will at times make you wonder if you're cut out to be a salesperson at all. Knowing when to close is as important as knowing how, as learned in the chapter on buying signals.

There are over forty useful closes that work in many situations. But if you are really concerned about solving your prospects' problems, you'll only need a few. Because if he thinks you're taking concerns off his worry list, he'll buy no matter what close you use. Unfortunately, many salespeople try to manipulate their prospect during the closing phase.

I recently spoke to an old-time sales pro who told me some techniques that he used to get people to buy. He said, "At the point I wanted to get that guy to sign the contract, I would take out my pen, show it's gold plating and flash it a couple of times in his eyes. I would then put the pen on the table, and let it roll down to the prospect, forcing him to take hold of it. At that point he would be compelled to sign the contract." Techniques like these are not only manipulative but also unethical. Not only will your prospect not buy, he will be insulted. There are many, many closing techniques that are not manipulative.

After you go through this chapter on closing, you will be able to close 30 percent more of your prospects, either on booking an appointment with you to see them face to face, or buying directly from you on the telephone. You'll close 30 percent more business just by using the right close with the right prospect.

## WHEN TO CLOSE

One key idea in knowing how to close is knowing when to close. The time your prospect should be closed is very critical. That time is when he wants to buy. Here's something for you to think about. Why not close your prospect when he wants to buy your product rather than when you want to sell? How often have you oversold your prospect in the past, by talking too long? Or frankly, you talked about a number of things your prospect didn't even care about, but you thought you had to say. Unfortunately, you're probably sabatoging yourself by talking about things your prospect does not care about.

The best time to close is after your prospect gives you a

verbal buying signal. These signals are given after you give key benefits. Your prospect may say, "Great, super, sounds wonderful," or in a more sophisticated vein, you will hear your prospect's voice modulate up. His voice pitch will go higher, "REALLY??"

Another way your prospect will give you a verbal buying signal is directly after he confirms that you have properly answered an objection. I found that the best time to close is directly after I present a key benefit matching my prospect's needs. In the chapter, "How to Discover Your Prospect's Buying Strategy," we discussed ways that you can actually find out how your prospect will buy. Once you find out his buying strategy, you can then literally present information the way he wants to hear it and close him the way he wants to be sold. For example, if your prospect told you that the last time he bought insurance was because it offered protection for the family, you realize that is still the most important thing to him. When you present to your prospect a better and newer way of adding protection for his family, you will close him. That is the single most important thing that he'll consider when he decides whether or not to buy your product. Above all, make sure you don't show hesitation if your prospect seems ready to buy. If you're like me, at least once, you've probably talked four or five minutes too long during a presentation.

I remember recently when all my staff were occupied on the telephone. I took a phone call from a gentleman requesting information about one of my tape cassette programs. He asked me a few questions about the programs and I probed him about his business. I then recommended the tape set I thought would be most appropriate to help him increase his production. At one point, I said, "This Psychology of Productivity tape program is guaranteed to increase your sales by 70 percent within six weeks." He said, "Super, sounds great to me." I then went on for at least five or six more minutes describing the reward-based psychological system that would help him increase not only activity but also production by at least 70 percent within six weeks. He then gave me an objection. He said, "Well, I think my activity is high enough as it is." When he said super and great, he was ready to buy. But because I gave him more information than was necessary, I actually talked him right past the close. I pushed him into giving more objections than he initially had. Don't do this to yourself. Give your buyer a chance to buy from you when he wants to, not when you want to sell.

One of the best times to close is directly after you receive an objection. If you remember the chapter on handling objections, you learned that if you're going to isolate an objection and answer it, the prospect will have absolutely no reason or excuse to say no to you. For example, if he says, "It's too much money," you could isolate that objection by saying, "Is that the only reason keeping you from going ahead with this right now?" If he said, "Yes, this is the only reason," and you answered it effectively, he logically will buy from you. Your response directly after he acknowledges that objection is overcome is, "Well let's do it," closing him. The only time you should not close after you answer an objection is on the telephone, especially within the first thirty seconds of the initial phone call. Your prospect may give you initial objections on the telephone like, "I'm too busy, I'm not interested, you telephone people call me all the time, would you leave me alone." This obviously is not the time to close because you were simply trying to keep yourself from getting blown off the telephone. But after you present your product in the way that your prospect wants to hear it, you better close or you will oversell yourself.

A secretary in my office once violated this rule and tried to close a prospect after an initial objection. She was following up with a referral that I had talked to a few years before. When he said, "We really never use outside speakers," she responded, "You want a great program, don't you?" The prospect said, "Of course, we want a good program." She then responded, "It's probably a good idea to use a professional speaker like Kerry Johnson. Would you like to use him for your April 17 meeting?" The prospect said no and almost hung up. You see, it's inappropriate to close that quickly because trust is not yet built up. If you already have trust and rapport you could close during the first ten seconds. But without these key ingredients, selling is as easy as walking through a brick wall.

## CLOSE THREE TIMES

Another rule of thumb in closing is to never give up until you have closed at least three times. This is a very important rule. Your prospect often may have a lack of self-confidence and may be simply frightened of buying. Often your prospect doesn't trust his own decisions. Be persistent, especially on the telephone, close on every call or appointment, but make sure you don't give up until you've tried to close three times.

If you're good on the telephone, as well as face-to-face, you probably have a goal on every call. Whether it is to get a referral or book a second appointment, or simply sell directly on the telephone, you should know what you want ahead of time. Expect to get objections. Expect the prospect to start out negatively and gradually warm up to you. But also expect that prospect to act like a pretty girl who already has a boyfriend. She keeps saying no, no, no, please don't, somemore. She actually wants you to give her attention and wants to say yes, but also wants you to be persistent. Prospects act absolutely the same way. They often want to block you to test your level of perseverance.

At a conference recently, I heard a top salesperson say that it takes actually five contacts to get a client or to sell a product. Five contacts over one, two, or three years, in my opinion, is a bit much. Instead, I think he was saying if you choose not to close a prospect, it will take you five contacts.

But if you attempt to close at least three times, your sale will certainly come sooner.

## TRANSFER URGENCY

Another rule of the closing road is to make sure you transfer a sense of urgency to your prospect. Your prospect absolutely will not buy if he doesn't sense there's a hurry. There are three reasons why your prospect may not buy: no need, no hurry, and no money. If you let your prospect take more time, he will procrastinate and will not buy. You've heard of Murphy's Law haven't you? It states that if anything can go wrong, it will go wrong. I believe in O'Toole's Law. O'Toole thought Murphy was an optimist. The Johnson Law states that if your prospect can find a way to put off a buying decision, he will. In my business, if I let a prospect procrastinate, there is only 5 percent chance he will buy later. That means ninety-five of the people that I'm not able to close right away will never buy.

Think what you can do to transfer a sense of urgency to your prospect. What can you give him to buy right now? Number one, offer discounts. If you have ever been solicited for a magazine subscription, you probably have heard the telemarketer say, "If you buy today, I'll give you twelve issues for the price of six, if you wait, you'll have to pay full retail price." Or, you can even transfer the idea that your prospect will lose benefits if he doesn't buy right now. Many salespeople say things like, "I'll give you free delivery if you buy today. I'll give you a package deal. You'll get a discount of 20 percent for everything."

Stockbrokers often cannot negotiate the price of the stock but they sure can negotiate the illusion of a loss. A stockbroker recently called me and said, "Dr. Johnson, sure you can wait until tomorrow, but there's some interesting news that came out today. This stock may go up by ten points between today and tomorrow. I can't promise that, but with the earnings published later today, I certainly see a strength in this issue." I kept thinking how much money I would lose by not buying that stock immediately. Many life insurance agents talk on the telephone and say things like, "If I can get you to move on this now, I can move this through underwriting more quickly. You know, of course, sir, that your policy is going to be very difficult to get through underwriting because of your heart attack. I can't make any guarantees but there is a very good chance that a gentleman I know in underwriting is working today. If I call him now, there is a good chance I can get this placed."

One insurance agent in the Midwest wrote me a letter saying he had problems with a prospect he couldn't get to buy. The prospect was procrastinating when the insurance agent said, "You know last year I had a prospect who decided to wait a little longer like you. He didn't think it was urgent to buy right away. In fact, after I was with him, I tried to help him buy, but he wanted to wait until the next month. The week after, he had a heart attack and died in his sleep. I'm not saying, Mr. Jones, that this is going to happen to you, but I'm certainly concerned about it." Will that work? You bet it will! It transfers urgency and motivation to your prospect. If he doesn't do it now, he may lose something, in this case his life.

Discounts are very effective if your company okays it. Before I bought my BMW, I looked at the car and then went home. The salesperson called me on the telephone that evening and said, "Listen if I throw the air-conditioning in, will you buy right now?" In my business, I get phone calls from people who want to buy tape programs. I often say to them, "Well, I realize you did not buy that tape cassette program at my speech last week. But if you buy right now, on the telephone, I will give you a free book and pay the postage; you will also receive a free newsletter." The bottom line is, don't let your prospect procrastinate. Make him risk a loss of a benefit if he waits. If you give your prospect a chance to procrastinate, he will. If your business is like mine, when he procrastinates he will rarely buy.

## BEST CLOSES TO USE

So far I've been discussing the best time to close and buying signals your prospects will typically give you. You should be asking yourself now, "Kerry, what is the best way to close?" In the following sections, I will give you a few tips and ideas on some very specific techniques that you could use to close more business than you've ever had before. Many sales trainers say the more closes you know, the more options and varieties you have to choose from to suit the situation. The closes I'm about to give you all fit very well into any situation you would like to plug them into. Some have better utility for the prospect who is difficult to deal with. Others have greater application by those prospects who are already in agreement. The most important thing is to practice these closes at least five times each to make them yours. If your close sounds contrived or canned, your prospect will know it right away.

### THE ASSUMPTIVE CLOSE

The *assumptive close* is built upon the idea that if your prospect doesn't stop you during the close, he's actually given his tacit consent to buy. Have you ever found a prospect in the past who seemed like he was afraid to actually say yes? Have you ever had a prospect who actually seemed like he wanted to be led by you into making a decision? Well, many of your prospects don't like to make decisions. They would rather you make the decision for them. "Mr. Jones, we've outlined your family's needs. Do you have time next Friday to pick up the car?" In this way the car salesman quickly progressed through the details and simply assumed the sale. The idea was that if the prospect didn't stop the salesperson, he owned the product.

Here's another example, "Mr, Thomas, this stock issue is a real winner. I'm going to put you down for a thousand shares so we can take advantage of this. Now what is the name of your bank again?" By telling your prospect what you're doing and then asking for the details, he very likely will go along with the flow. My wife, Sandy, and I recently bought a house. The realtor we were dealing with explained how much the house cost and asked if we would like to make an offer. I hemmed and hawwed and avoided making a decision. Then she pulled out the offer sheet and asked me how to spell my first name. She actually filled out the sheet without formally asking me if I'd like to buy the house. This eventually led to the offer price. You know what? She did get an offer from me. I thought, "What the heck, I like the house. I'll make a really low offer and see if they accept it." It wasn't accepted the first time. But I got caught up in the sales negotiation and made another offer that was acccepted.

Nobody likes to run headlong into an oncoming train. When you do an assumptive close, you're actually saying to your prospect, "I'm going to help you buy. I'm going to do everything for you in making this decision so you don't even have to make the effort to say yes. Just don't stop me." I was closed recently on the telephone by a fundraiser for a public television station in this way. The gentleman who talked to me explained what he wanted and probed me. He explained his need for money to keep the local station alive. He asked me where I lived, I told him. He was familiar with my area. He then asked, "You live in Woodbridge, don't you?" I said yes. He then said, "With your income, I'm going to put you down for five hundred dollars per year as a donation. What's your wife's name?" He reconfirmed my address and then hung up. The idea behind the assumptive close is that your prospect will buy unless he stops you. It is probably one of the two best closes that you can ever use. It'll work in almost every situation in which you sense the prospect is avoiding a decision. I use it more than any other close because I don't want the prospect to get a chance to say no.

## MINOR AGREEMENT CLOSE

This close is predicated on the idea that if you can get your prospect to give you a series of yeses, he will buy from you. It's called the *minor agreement close*. The strategy behind this is to actually get your prospect to make a series of small decisions. The momentum your prospect displays in making those small decisions will culminate in making a big decision to buy the product. In other words, if you can get your prospect involved in making minor decisions, he will make a major decision later without thinking much about it. That means decision time will go down. That means the number of objections you receive will go down just as readily. I was recently closed by a telephone discount service salesperson. He said during the presentation, "You probably want a free credit card don't you?" I said, "Yes. I guess I do want that." He added, "Oh, by the way, you also probably want a 35 percent discount during the day, correct?" I said, "Yes." He said, "Okay, I'll see if I can hook you up by Friday." Now this telephone salesperson had probed my telephone usage. But during the time that he presented, he actually bypassed the stage of telling me what his telephone system cost and immediately asked me questions leading up to the sale. Now to be honest with you, I did give this individual an objection. I said, "Wait a minute, not so fast, tell me more about your company. He could have just as readily presented the company and then asked me a series of minor questions to try to grab my interest. Nonetheless, this is an extremely effective technique.

I once was asked by a travel agent who was trying to sell

me a European vacation, "You want to go to Europe this summer, correct?" "Yes." She added, "How much are you prepared to spend?" I answered, "Oh, about a thousand dollars." "I can get you to Waterloo, Iowa, for a thousand dollars. Where would you like to go?" I gave her an itinerary of the locations I wanted to visit. She asked, "Do you want to stay at the Savoy in London?" I realized how expensive it was. I gave her an objection and said, "That's a little too expensive for my taste. What else have you got?" So you see, not all small agreements will end up in a sale for you. These agreements must be things that your prospect will typically say yes to, not major decisions. The Savoy was a major decision. For example, my financial planner once said in selling an investment, "Kerry, you want high growth on your money right?" "Of course." "You want a 9 percent cash flow?" "You got it." "You want quarterly dividends don't you?" "Yeah." "Then let's get you into this XYZ Fund." When he said, "I'm going to put ten thousand dollars into this XYZ Fund," I bought from him on the spot.

## THE LITTLE EXTRA CLOSE

Have you ever noticed that the best time to close a prospect is directly after he has already bought? Your toughest job is to get the prospect to say yes and make a decision. After he makes a major decision, getting him to buy something else is child's play, if you have more than one product. Why only sell one? Why not sell both to the same prospect? He will be most receptive to you directly after he has bought something. After your prospect has bought, don't be afraid of then selling an add-on product. For example, if your prospect just bought a life insurance policy, you might talk next about disability. If your prospect just bought a stock or bond over the telephone, you might quickly discuss mutual funds directly afterward. Have you noticed that when you book a hotel room, you're often asked right away if you need a car? After you book an airline reservation, the salesperson will say, "Do you need a car rental when you get there?" It's often difficult to get people to buy initially, it is often easy to get them to make another buying decision. It's not very difficult. What's difficult is to get your prospect to change his mind with another product. Let me give you an example of this. Recently an executive with a financial company in Wisconsin asked me to speak at his conference. The executive said, "We would like you to speak on Saturday morning at nine." When we consummated the deal, I told him I would send him an agreement. But before I got off the telephone I said, "By the way, this group also has a spouses' meeting as well, is that true?" He said, "Yes we do." I asked, "Why not let me do another program on stress for the spouses later on that day? Have you got plans so far for them?" He said, "Well, we were going to take them shopping but that is a good idea." I said, "I'm going to be there anyway. You would certainly save on airfare." He said, "Sounds good to me, let's do it." In that way I doubled my speaking fee just by following up and suggesting another product. If you have another product available why not sell? It's the best time for them to buy.

## ALTERNATE OF CHOICE CLOSE

In my opinion, the three best closes to use are, the assumptive close, the "I recommend" close, and the alternate of choice close. The latter close is an extremely effective close because your prospects have a tendency to focus directly on simplistic choices. They tend to keep very few options and alternatives in their minds at once. They tend to think of your product in very simplistic terms. Those choices are basically should I buy or not? Should I see that person on a face-to-face appointment or not? Should I buy one or two? This is an important facet of human behavior. We really crave simple choices. Give your prospect what she wants. Give her a simple choice as part of a close. When my daughter, Stacy, was young, like many two year olds, she wanted to play with things she was not allowed to touch. One day she grabbed an expensive vase. When I tried to take it out of her hand, she screamed and yelled. Being an indulgent father, I tried to placate Stacy to avoid hearing her cry. I decided to use an alternate of choice close. I said, "Would you like a doll or a game to play with?" I sidetracked Stacy to choose her doll and she gave me the vase. You can't totally change the subject with your prospect but you certainly can give him choices of what to buy. Instead of offering your prospect a yes or no to your question, why not instead ask him if he wants a thousand or fifteen hundred units to start. "Is $550,000 or $600,000 of this limited partnership more attractive right now, Mr. Prospect?" You can even use this technique with appointments. Should we meet Tuesday at 4:15 or Wednesday at 5:45?

One important thing to remember is that you should try not to mix choices and benefits together. The whole idea of the alternate of choice is to be simplistic. If you complicate by mixing choices and benefits, it will lose its effect and your prospect will become confused. For example, one way of mixing benefits and choices is to say to your prospect, "Mr. Jones, should we meet Tuesday at 4:45 at your office or Wednesday at 5:45 at Mimi's restaurant." This alternate of choice technique may confuse your prospect instead of keeping him focused on one choice.

I recently bought a few tennis racquets from a company specializing in mail order equipment. After reading *Tennis* magazine, I called a phone number in the magazine and asked the salesperson how much the racquets cost. She said, "$49." I said, "Well, I'll get back to you after I talk to my wife." The lady wisely understood that if she let me off the telephone, I would never buy. She said instead, "Well, we're almost out of these tennis racquets. The manufacturer has discontinued the line. We only have a few left. Would you like three or four racquets?" I bought four. She actually turned me from a prospect who was moderately interested into a proud owner of four new Head Edgwood tennis racquets.

## THE COMPROMISE CLOSE

Have you ever been very close to making a sale, but to your surprise your prospect gave you an objection such as, "I need to talk to my accountant," or, "I need to talk to my wife?" Sometimes when your prospect is just on the threshold to buying, he can be prompted to say yes by a very effective negotiation technique called the *compromise close*. Here's how it works. Rather than trying to get your prospect to buy everything that you want him to buy, compromise a little bit. Don't expect as much from your prospect; get him to make a smaller investment at first.

The way to compromise close is first try to close the normal way. If you get an objection you can't handle, try to re-establish agreement with what your prospect wants. Try instead to say to that prospect, "Well, I think you mentioned that you did want to buy a tax shelter this month, correct?" Make sure you reaffirm your prospects goals and desires. Then compromise with your prospect by getting him to make a smaller initial investment. Say for example, "Mr. Jones, I understand that you need to run this by your accountant, but do you agree that this seems like a good investment and generally fits your financial objectives?" "Well, I guess, I do. But I still need to run this by my accountant." "Does the investment seem too big for you right now?" "Yes." "Mr. Jones, rather than lose this opportunity, let's make a partial investment of only a thousand shares rather than the initial five thousand we talked about." The premise is that if you think your prospect is very close to buying but is stalling and giving you an objection you can't handle, you must realize that if he takes a while to think about it, he will procrastinate and never buy. Instead, get him to agree to a lesser sale. This is especially important on the telephone. If you're selling paper clips, and trying to push that prospect to buy ten thousand boxes, decrease it to five thousand boxes if you think you're close, anyway. Negotiators use compromises frequently. They try to make negotiation a win/win situation as often as possible. They frequently know that they can't always have everything they want, but at the same time, they get most of what they want. Salespeople should act and react the same way.

## THE RECOMMEND CLOSE

Have you ever noticed that physicians have nearly a 100 percent closing rate? In a year you may spend hundreds or even thousands of dollars just on getting the advice of physicians, largely because of the amount of respect you put in them. The attitude you probaby have is, "Well, he's the doctor, he should know." But in effect, doctors are very often wrong. Their advice is faulty. That is why we are encouraged to get second opinions, especially in complex cases. One of the reasons we so freely accept the advice of the physician is because he uses a technique called the "I recommend" close. It works like this. "Mr. Jones, based on what I heard so far about your requirements for durability and budget constraints, I recommend our new 335 copier. It will give you the specifications you require as well as still fit within your budget. Would you like to finance it with a loan plan or pay cash?" This recommend close, as you can tell, was combined with the alternate of choice close. You can often combine two closes and get very good results.

I once was called by a magazine telemarketer who said, "Dr, Johnson, based on your interest in tennis and world events, I recommend *Tennis World* magazine and also *Newsweek*." The reason this close works well is because you listen well. If you do not probe well, you cannot use this close. But if you probe effectively, your prospect will immediately assume that you listened so well that you gave your professional opinion and advice in recommending a product or service. The reason this close works for physicians in getting you to pay for high-priced surgery, drugs, and therapies is because they diagnosed you effectively. You put your trust in them and their diagnosis because they took a long time listening to you talk about your symptoms. When they recommend a course of action, you took their advice.

I said before that this is my favorite close. It's probably more effective for me than the assumptive or alternate of choice. I like to listen and probe my prospects well especially when I first talk to them. I don't let prospects ramble, but when I hear enough, I will stop them and say, "I understand that you want more production, more incentives and more productivity, that's why I recommend......" I suppose one of the reasons this works so well for me is because I let the prospects know that I listened and know their goals. I repeat their goals during the presentation stage and simply say, "I recommend you take this course of action." Unless they trust their own diagnosis more than mine, they will typically do what I recommend.

## YES, NO CLOSE

Have you ever had a prospect, especially on the telephone, who seemed to waste your time? You called him a few times and just couldn't get him to commit. I know that this happens in my business. We have prospects we talked to on the telephone for sometimes two or three years. They never seem to commit to using my services. We have a rule in my office that states, either close it or forget it. We follow up with prospects and give them a chance to buy eventually, but just like your business, 20 percent of the people we contact give us 80 percent of our revenues. We want to try to clear out those individuals who are just wasting our time. Our files show that we often talk to prospects at least once every six months. Certainly we don't contact them once a day, or even once a month. We do communicate with them sometimes five to ten times without their ever saying yes.

Would you like to find a technique that will work to either push your prospect to say yes or clear him out? Here's a sentence you might consider asking your prospect, "Mr. Jones, we talked a couple of times now about this donation to the Child Security Fund. I really need a yes or no right now whether you want to contribute to help us solve these problems." It's best, as you can see, to attach a strong benefit to the end of the statement. There's always that chance that you literally may be able to shock your prospect into a yes by letting him know that you're not going to spend any more time with him. He will lose the chance of buying the product if he stalls any longer. Obviously this is also a bit of a last resort close. But doesn't it make sense that getting no's is better than wasting more of your time. Remember the difference between love and hate? It's much better to get a negative from your prospect than disinterest.

I once worked with a group of stockbrokers and frankly told them to look at all their files and clear out those prospects who had not bought a product in the last year. Stockbrokers often do a very good job of following up. But sometime even they spend time trying to contact prospects who never will buy anything. It is very, very difficult to clear out clients with whom a stockbroker has a good rapport. But I asked these stockbrokers to make one statement, "Mr. Jones, our records show that you have not made a transaction with us in the last nine months. Would you mind if I tossed your file away?" You know what happened? Out of those people who have not bought in months, a full 50 percent, said, "Please don't throw my file away." They then made a purchase. Fifty percent of those individuals who were contacted actually felt so uneasy about having their record tossed away that they tried to keep the relationship strong by buying something. They didn't want to lose the opportunity of working with that stockbroker. You might want to consider this technique with those prospects you're not getting through to. Realize that there's a certain amount of follow-up that needs to be done with some prospects while others may simply take your time and waste it. Take the attitude, "I'm going to cut my losses and work on somebody else. Either buy or get out." You'll be suprised at the results you get.

## PAUSE CLOSE

There is another close called the *pause close*. Sometimes a prospect who is uncomfortable with silence will actually let you make use of that silence. That prospect, when you try to close him, will actually be so uncomfortable with silence that at the point that you close, he will try to fill that void. For example, mention during the close, "You can get a 20 percent discount and free delivery." Then pause directly afterwards. You will make that prospect sufficiently uncomfortable that he will give a response. The unfortunate thing is, he may say no and give you an objection, but he is very likely to say yes.

## IF I COULD WOULD YOU CLOSE

Some of your prospects are enormously good negotiators. When they sense the approach of the closing phase, they will actually try to get more out of you. They realize that they might be able to get you to lower your price or give extra benefits. Sometimes, for example, those individuals who buy consumer goods, like T.V.s, stereos or video players, will get very close to saying yes, but then try a better deal. They'll go to your competitor and say, "Look at what he's giving me.

Can you beat it?"

Have you ever heard before, "Well, I'd like to buy this, but first, can you give me a 10 percent discount? You can? Great, I'll call you back later if I decide to buy." So the objective is to turn a request for compromise for extra benefits into a closing opportunity. Instead of answering the question of whether you could get a 10 percent discount, say to that prospect, "Well, Mr. Jones, if I could give a 10 percent discount, would you buy today? If I could deliver it for free would you make your purchase today? Mr. Jones, if I could save you $300 on airfare would you make your decision right now?" If that prospect says no, then the obvious response you would be, "My goal Mr. Jones, is to give you what you want. What is most important to you?" The objective in this case is simply not to let your prospect get the best deal in town and then procrastinate. Your objection is to get him to buy.

## APPOINTMENT CLOSES

Up until now, I've talked about general closing techniques. But now let's get more specific on booking appointments on the telephone. Appointments are often as difficult to gain on the telephone as closing a prospect face-to-face. The best closes to use on gaining an appointment are the assumptive, alternate of choice close, and the "I recommend" close. You may even wish to use a combination of these closes.

When I first started consulting, I made cold calls in California from a directory called, *Contacts Influential*. This is a listing of businesses by industry. It lists all the real estate companies within a given location, as well as insurance companies and even accounting firms. I was taught by a colleague of mine to book appointments by using the alternate of choice close. I would open with, "Hi, Mr. Jones, my name is Kerry Johnson, I want to talk to you about helping your sales people increase production. I would like to see you next Tuesday at

3:30 or is 4:00 better?" Most of my prospects would say, "No, I'm not interested." One prospect, after about two weeks of calling said, "Boy, I know what you're trying to do. I'm a salesman too." He obviously thought I was being manipulative. He realized that I was new and closed inappropriately. What I neglected to do was get rapport on the cold call, ask questions, and probe. Most importantly, I needed to present a couple of grabber benefits in an effort to close that prospect on allowing me to see him face-to-face.

One rule I always had, and I hope you agree with, is never allow your prospect to call you back regarding an appointment. You'll never get it. If you do reach that individual on the telephone, don't allow him to say to you, "Well, I'll have to check my schedule and call you back," or, "I'll have my secretary call you back when I'm free." You'll never get that appointment. Instead, make a tentative time. "Mr. Jones, I realize that you don't have your calendar in front of you right now, but just to make a tentative time, how about Thursday at 4:00 until you get a chance to get back to me?"

The best technique to gain an appointment is to first develop high rapport. If you've got rapport, business will come to you. If you do not have rapport, you will not possess the currency of interpersonal relationships. If your prospect senses that you care about him, closing him will be much easier. He will sense either manipulation or your sincere desire to help him. Low-rapport salespeople close between one and two prospects out of every twenty. High-rapport salespeople often find that their closing rate is as much as five to ten times that. The best example of manipulation in closing I can give you is the story of how lions hunt. You probably know that the breadwinner in a lion family is the lioness. She is the one who actually hunts the prey, kills it, and brings it back to the rest of the family. What the male lion typically does is sleep all day. What a great life they have, huh? There are often antelope nearby on which the lion preys. Even if the lioness is upwind from the antelope, smell alone will not prompt the antelope to flee. When the lion family is fed they will lay around or even walk without disturbing the antelope. But when the lion family grows hungry, and the lioness decides it's her time to hunt, even a flick of her eyebrow or a slight ruffle of her fur will send the antelope scurrying away for miles. It's not just the approaching danger that causes fear in the antelope, it's the look of the predator. It's the message transmitted by very slight verbal and non-verbal cues that lets the antelope know the lioness is hunting, and no longer just "hanging around."

It is the same antelope-lioness connection that you have with your prospect. Your prospect is the antelope, you are the lioness. If you look like you're a predator, your prospect will feel like the hunted and will not buy from you. It will be very difficult to probe effectively because you will have no trust. On the other hand, if it appears to your prospect that you want to help rather than take something from him, he will work very hard in giving you what you want.

Using these closing techniques will undoubtedly help you sell more effectively. This is part of the overall sequence of closing a greater amount of business. In other words, help your prospect make decisions; allow your prospect to buy more quickly.

In the next section, we'll learn how managers can develop people who produce. In the following chapter, you'll learn how to analyze and improve your management performance.

# 4

---

# HOW TO DEVELOP PEOPLE WHO WILL PRODUCE

# PART 21

# BUILDING YOUR MANAGEMENT SKILLS

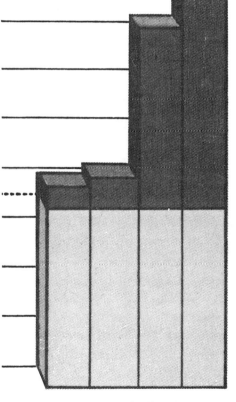

Have you ever met a manager who was "misleading?" Possibly you have worked with a manager who shot from the hip? Have you dealt with an associate who procrastinated making decisions, or was so bureaucratic that he always went, *"by the book?"*

Many managers know theories of management and do an inadequate job in the practical application of this knowledge. They have learned how to plan, organize, motivate, and control. Yet they are missing the real point of effective management. *Peak performing managers manage things and lead people.* The missing link in theory is that great managers know how to manage technically and, more importantly, possess an ability to apply the right management style at the right time.

A small distribution company was headed by an owner who was frustrating his staff and salespeople. He was an entrepreneurial free spirit who had started his business from scratch and prided himself on being a persuasive idea man. He said some of his best ideas came during his commute to and from the office. Unfortunately for his staff, his *"best ideas"* came daily if not hourly. First, his staff would work on activities such as improving direct mail pieces. Then the owner would develop sophisticated marketing techniques. With each new piece of creativity would come an equally new direction. He possessed a management style that was inappropriate for his already established business. What should he have done? Read on. . .

## ROLES OF MANAGEMENT

An effective manager possesses four crucial characteristics. He is a *producer*. He is achievement oriented, insuring that the mission of the organization is carried out. The objective of a company is rarely to produce profits. Instead, it's mission is to deliver a product or service that the buyer values. The manager as a *producer* focuses on this as his duty to the organization. His concern is to achieve bottom line results.

Next, a manager is an *administrator*. He controls the machinery of his organization to insure that the system is well greased and functions according to design. He focuses on scheduling, coordinating, and keeping the business running efficiently.

A manager also is an *entrepreneur*. He gives direction and must be able to set goals as well as aid in policy making. He must be a self-starter and a risk-taker who is willing, if necessary, to change direction in mid-stream.

Lastly, a manager is an *integrator*. He takes independent-minded people and coalesces them into a harmonious team. This management component is essential in helping the business function in unison without an overdependency on any one individual.

## THE LONE AVENGER

Unfortunately, although many managers have more than one of these leadership characteristics, they may exhibit only one to any degree. For example, the manager whose primary style is to produce results without commensurate abilities to utilize the other components is called the *Lone Avenger.* *The Lone Avenger* has a high level of achievement in carrying out decisions. He is knowledgeable and sees what needs to be done and how it should be done. He often is so busy producing that he forgets to encourage the development of those around him. He doesn't delegate well because he believes he can do the work better and faster himself. His long-range planning is limited to next week. He is busy doing, doing, doing.

Don, a manager I met recently, fits this mold. He works twelve hour days in his financial planning practice. Don feels good when friends tell him he works too hard. His desk is piled with client folders marked "A" priority, while a secretary types up directions for a meeting thirty days hence. His staff act like an audience watching a performance. He told me at lunch that he wants to replace them. "They don't do anything right," he stated. I asked if he spent time training them. He said he didn't have the time.

## THE BUREAUCRAT

The controller or administrator component characteristic by itself is called the *Bureaucrat.* This is the detail person who makes sure the system runs efficiently. However, the *Bureaucrat* is not results or change oriented. He "goes by the book" and is often the one in the company who will reject new ideas. He is overly organized and conservative, frequently complaining about violations of rules or procedures. Praise to staff members is proffered for the way activities are handled rather than for results achieved. He prides himself on the level of harmony and control in the office.

Recently, I was invited by a vice president of marketing to speak at a sales incentive conference in Bermuda. After learning how much I charge, he said he'd have to clear it with another executive. He also asked if I would like to speak with the executive. I called the executive and told him of the vice president's plans. He was clearly disturbed, and said, "Why does he always do that to me? We've already got the meeting organized and he's trying to change it and go beyond our budget. I'll talk to him." Needless to say, the project was killed. What was surprising was that the vice president was both angered by and afraid of the Bureaucrat.

## THE FIRESTARTER

The *Entrepreneur* is the idea man of the organization. He is the person expected to furnish insight into organizational direction. This behavioral component of management functions as the change agent of the business, often instigating controversy and initiating policy. He must be innovative, and excels in coming up with ideas and creating new projects. He is enthusiastic, stimulating, and exciting. His complaints usually center on those who don't understand his priorities. He hires those who support him enthusiastically and seem to admire him. He also is likely to dismiss those who do not match his level of enthusiasm.

Mark, the owner of a training and development company, fits this stereotype. Charismatic and enthusiastic, he will travel for a week or two at a time, talking with clients and getting great new ideas. When he returns to his office, he puts pressure on his staff, overloading them with assignments to gather information for his use, only to change direction again. He doesn't set new priorities, he instead sets additional ones.

Mark is feared by his staff, not because of his attitude, but because they know when he is in the office, the whirlwind of crisis will begin. He often assigns two or three project development ideas at once, but doesn't get involved in follow through or details since he sees himself as a "big picture person." He has positively no idea of how the business runs on a day-to-day basis.

## THE THERAPIST

The fourth component of effective organizational management is the *Integrator*, the one who helps the others coalesce into a team. He brings people together and facilitates consensus or compromise in solving problems. By himself he excels at getting agreement from others. He judges his own effectiveness by the role he plays in working out important problems and resolving struggles. He makes decisions only when everyone is in agreement, and is disappointed when staff members don't get along. He tends to hire people who are submissive and seem to be as sensitive and people oriented as he is. His staff meetings are loosely organized, and he allows people to talk about anything they like.

One example of an integrator is an executive I know, an ex-Catholic priest who decided that business is more his cup of tea. He is concerned about people and dislikes pressuring them to produce results. He was once shown a method he could use to increase his salespeople's production, (it involved a rigorous use of rewards and punishments), he refused the technique saying he wanted them to develop their own rewards. His staff enjoys his easy demeanor. He is likable, but lacks the bottom-line orientation characteristic of some of his associates.

## THE ANSWER

The answer to developing a perfect manager is. . . there is no answer. An equal proportion of producer, administrator, entrepreneur, and integrator is so rare in an individual manager that looking for one would be a futile exercise. Rarely does a manager possess only one of these characteristics. Frequently, he will display all of these traits in varying degrees, depending upon the situation. Therefore, it is the business need that dictates which management style will be applicable. The unique needs or level of maturity of the individual determines which personal management style should be utilized.

The stage of development of your company will yield information on how you should manage. In the illustration that follows, you'll see the stages of business growth.

## STAGES OF BUSINESS DEVELOPMENT

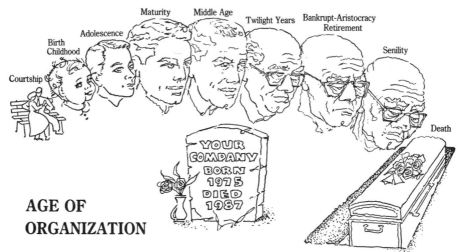

AGE OF
ORGANIZATION

The first step, or *courtship*, is the dream stage. The founders are selling the idea to others as a way of testing the validity of their own inspirations. This step requires that participants be primarily entrepreneurial. Although the producer, administrator and integrator skills are also required to some extent, the central focus is on the entrepreneurial component.

Production begins at *birth*. Payroll is under way and monthly needs must be met. The producer characteristic becomes necessary to produce results from an idea that may have been written on the back of an envelope. The other behavioral components are utilized, but the producer becomes king.

In *childhood,* the organization has the same production needs, but it also requires vision. The producer and the entrepreneur share the perch at the top. The organization is growing rapidly, and everybody does everything from acting as designer to accountant to chief bottle washer.

In *adolescence,* the administrative role takes on more prominence, sharing top influence with the insighted entrepreneurs. In healthy *adolescence,* the business moves from crisis into organization, often doing so at the expense of sales. However, the greater need for administration will insure long-term success.


## BELL CURVE PEAK

In the *mature* organization, the producer, administrator and entrepreneur share equal influence and responsibility. Crises are kept to a minimum, and the organization is able to effectively support what it sells. The rate of growth is stable and predictable. Integration is still not high because of the necessity of the visionary entrepreneur.

The *middle-aged* organization is high in production, administration, and integration, but low on entrepreneurs. It is well organized and result oriented, but creativity is short lived. People spend more time in the office than with customers. There is less concern for long-term growth and survival than short-term profits for the stockholders.


## DECLINE

Throughout the twilight years into *senility,* the business slowly allows the creative entrepreneurial characteristic to atrophy. The producer is gradually strangled by the heightened power of the administrator, until the operation is living off the old revenues while slowly dying due to loss of progressive new ideas and products. If it is to survive and go back to it's prime state, it must purchase a younger and more enlightened company to pass the baton to.

## REGENERATION

To keep this organization from dying a premature death, it must bring out the talents of the producer, entrepreneur, administrator, and integrator when needed. To administer prematurely would cause a halt in sales; to do it too late would deal a blow to customer service. The real challenge is to use the appropriate management styles in the right blend at the optimal organizational maturity level. This will help your organization thrive in even the toughest of times. Balance is achieved when all components — entrepreneur, producer, administrator, and integrator — interact like parts of a finely tuned machine.

Create a full-component and managerial system, and reap the benefits of functioning at the peak of the bell curve. You will be guaranteed a vital and successful long-lasting organization.

In the next chapter, we'll look at ways of interviewing to choose the right candidates for employment in your company.

# PART 22

---

# INTERVIEWING FOR THE TRUTH

In the dirty wartorn streets of Beirut, one views a battlefield of destruction. Devastated by decades of war, the inhabitants consist of combatants fighting for and against an embattled country. Strategies of urban guerrilla warfare dictate not only fighting against Muslim and Christian enemies, but also taking hostages. Numerous kidnapped Americans have been held for months, some even years. The CIA, charged with rescuing these innocent victims, has employed a tenuous network of informants to observe and listen. Often, the information they report back is unconfirmed. The CIA has not been able to rely on the paid informants' stories until now.

Unable to carry a lie detector in the field for fear of blowing their cover, CIA operatives are armed with a technique for uncovering the truth, or at least what the informant believes to be the truth. According to a former intelligence agency consultant based in Long Beach, California, the CIA has developed a single yet reliable method of gaining the truth by observing the informant's eyes. If the informant moves his eyes in the correct direction, the interviewer knows he is to be believed.

## THE RESEARCH

Researchers at the University of California in Santa Cruz have discovered that eye movement can be an indication of shyness, but also representative of the truth. Human beings are born with intricate thought processes that are not always mysterious. Business educators traditionally have recommended good eye contact in an attempt to facilitate trust between partners. Unfortunately, they have not yielded much information about what to detect in the gaze. According to researchers, when people look to their left while contemplating, they are recalling information. They are trying to remember information they have seen or heard previously. When looking to their left, they may be trying to recall an incident while answering a question. These people may be in the process of hearing a past conversation or remembering an image. For example, in interviewing a new salesperson to hire, you may ask the question, "Tell me about your last job." If the recruit looks to his left, he is probably recalling a picture of his past associate's business, looking at the office setting. The recruit might say, "I was in charge of marketing for a small manufacturing company."

The same researchers have also determined that eye movement to the right is an indication of future thoughts. When your interviewee looks to the right, he may be creating pictures of how things should be or hearing future sounds. Often when interviewing, managers ask about the financial needs of their recruits. For example, to the question, "How much money would you like to make," the recruit may look to his right. In this case, he may be envisioning a dream house for his family. Not yet built, he may be constructing future sounds of his wife's verbal ecstasy when he tells her he found a career that will provide the funds. He may say, "I guess I need $3,000 a month to build our new house next year."

## INTERVIEW FOR THE TRUTH

The key to finding the truth is to not only listen but also to watch. The CIA has learned, according to reliable sources, that if their informant is asked a question about what he saw or heard in the past and he creates or constructs pictures or sounds of what to say, he is lying. If you ask your applicant if he has ever had sales experience and he looks to his right, he may be fabricating a story for your benefit. If your question is meant to gain accurate information from the past and he instead gives you the future, he may be telling what you want to hear instead of the facts.

Side Right          Side Left

Recently, I spoke to a group of managers in Atlanta at a conference. I brought a member of the audience up to test this concept. I asked about his vacation. He said he went to Hawaii last year and stayed at the Hyatt on the island of Maui. When I asked about his activities, the manager said he and his wife went scuba diving. At that point, I noticed that his gaze went to the right. I stopped him and asked, "Are you sure about that?" Embarrassed and amused, he admitted that only his wife went scuba diving. He just laid around soaking up the sun on the beach. I could hear laughter from the more than 100 attendees in the audience.

Quicker than a lie detector test, this technique of watching eyes will give you enormous power during an interview. No longer do you have to trust that what you hear to be the truth. You now are armed with a tool which will give you an inside advantage in predicting whether your candidate will succeed in your business. You will gain information about their real past instead of what they think you want to hear.

## WHAT TO ASK

As exception to the eyes right-create, eyes left-recall, rule of thumb involves left handed people. Because of brain physiology, 10 to 12 percent of these left-handed folk will switch, giving you false readings. The best way to determine this discrepancy is to ask about their birthplace. Most people have little incentive to lie about where they were born. But this question will also help you adapt to your interviewee's eye patterns. Simply ask, "Tom, where were you raised?" If Tom looks to the right creatively and says, "Chicago," check to see if he is left handed. If he is right handed, ask the question again. The next time he might say, "Evanston, near Chicago." Technically, a lie, Tom may instead have been trying to save you time wondering where Evanston is. His mind searched for the largest nearby city.

Your recruits often don't mean to lie. They may simply fabricate in an effort to make memories complete. My wife asked me recently why I was late for dinner. I looked to the left and said, "I'm sorry I'm late, I got a phone call just as I was walking out the door." She said, "Who was it?" I said, "My travel agent." Unfortunately, my wife Sandy knows too much about this eye movement research. She saw me look to the right as I answered her question. She angrily said, "All right, smart guy, what were you really doing?" I couldn't remember exactly so I gave her a quick answer. I recall working on flight plans with someone, so it must have been my travel agent.

Lie detectors operate on the assumption that human beings know that it is wrong to lie. When we say something wrong or untruthful, we encounter stress. Polygraph machines are designed to pick up that stress. But in an interview, you should not be as concerned about whether your recruit has a police record as whether he will succeed as a sales or marketing pro. The questions you ask are designed to uncover any problem areas or strengths the candidate may possess. It is crucial that you determine the truth as he knows it.

The St. Paul Insurance Companies are currently using this truth test in loss prevention programs as well as with claims from policy holders. According to an industrial psychologist I interviewed, they have realized a surprising decrease in unverifiable claims in the property and casualty operations ("Mr. Jones, I noticed you looked to your right when you said the building ran into your car. How did that happen?").

One manager using this technique recently tested it with exciting results. One of his recruits was showing signs of stress in an interview. The candidate rubbed his forehead, blinked his eyes rapidly, and fidgeted. The manager asked, "What does your wife think of your new career move?" As his eyes moved side right, he said, "She's all for anything that makes me happy." The perceptive manager replied, "But she isn't behind you 100 percent on this, is she?" The interviewee this time looked left and said, "Well to tell you the truth, she wants me to go to work for my father, but I'm just not happy in his business." A sales career is difficult during the first few years, even with the strong support of a spouse. Without that support, the difficulties may be insurmountable. This simple interview tool enabled the manager to probe more deeply into a possible problem area that could have hurt his prospective employee's chances for success.

Watch your recruit's eyes as well as listen to their words. What they say is not always what they mean. *More impor-*

*tantly, what they say is not all that they mean.* If you can improve your interview skills and select better people, you will strengthen your business. This tool will help. Eyes will tell you a lot if you know how to read them. After all, they are the windows to the soul. In the next chapter, we'll discuss the art (and benefits) of praise.

# PART 23

## PRAISE: DEVELOPING SUPER-STARS

John was excited about his first job. He worked hard the first few months to learn necessary skills. He wanted to do the best job he could and hoped to come up with some ideas to increase his productivity. During the first months he received little, if any feedback. He was given only minimal direction and supervision. Finally, plagued with frustration, he went to his supervisor, Tom Grant. "Mr. Grant, how am I doing? I really want to do well in this job. I receive all the help I need, but I don't have any feeling as to whether I am doing well or not. Help me." Mr. Grant's gruff response was, "You're doing just fine, John. I'll let you know if you're not."

Unfortunately, too many businesses are run this way. The only time the supervisor gives you feedback is when you are making mistakes, instead of tearing John's self-esteem apart and leaving him in a motivational limbo state, Mr. Grant, with a little praise and a few kind words, could have given John the inspiration he wanted to keep doing well.

## THE NEED FOR REWARDS

Our day-to-day activities reflect a high desire to receive a reward or avoid punishment. You may think this is pretty obvious. However, remember that people need praise for their efforts just as they need air.

If you want someone to develop a skill, praise them for it first. Comment on one activity that the person does well and is similar to the new activity you wish them to learn. My tennis coach at the University of California at San Diego was a master at using praise to develop skills. He would compliment an aspect of my game with such tact that I was compelled to concentrate on making it still better. During a practice match, when my serve was a bit erratic, the coach walked over to me and said, "I really like your ball toss. It's hitting right on the money." That bit of praise made me feel good, but more importantly, forced me to concentrate on the things I was doing right instead of on the things I was doing wrong.

You may be thinking, "My employees don't do anything worth praising!" If you look really hard (perhaps when they aren't watching) you might be able to catch them in the act of doing something right. Compliment them on the action right then and there. One member of my staff had a very difficult time adapting to a new computer I purchased for the office. She was scared to death of the machine and couldn't relax enough to operate it. Whenever I asked her to bring up a file onto the screen, she invariably ended up erasing the program. I was sure she had computerphobia. My goal, however, was to get her to do word processing efficiently within thirty days. That was a fairly difficult goal for someone who dreamed nightly of shooting the computer with a bazooka!

I began by praising her for the actions she did right. She was stroked for putting the floppy disk into the drive, right side up. After a few days of praising, she learned to type a business letter and store it correctly onto the disk. Since this was graduation day, I took her to lunch. Finally, I maintained her new-found skill by randomly praising her when she correctly operated the system. Several months later, she confided to me that she expended extra effort to learn how to use the computer because of the strokes I gave her as she progressed. She admitted that the praise she received was even a more effective motivator than money. I built her self-esteem as well as motivation level.

Technically, this is called *successive approximation.* Psychologists have known for years that an acrophobic shouldn't be taken skydiving the first day out. But instead, her fears should be overcome in small steps by first looking at airplane pictures, then progressing up to actually sitting in an airplane.

*Stroke people at least twice a day.* It is, of course, preferable to link the compliments to skills you would like them to develop or repeat. Even a comment about their appearance that day or the neatness of their work station will help. But, don't fall into the trap of being critical at the expense of reward. Criticism is a punishment people try to avoid. People often develop resentment when they are criticized. The process of praising others twice a day will also push you to find praise-worthy actions.

Studies done at Stanford University showed that chimpanzees would learn to ride tricycles with either praise (kind words and a treat) or criticism (yelling). However, the chimps who received shouts for mistakes bared their teeth, screamed, and avoided the trainer whenever possible. The chimps receiving punishment were also more difficult to teach other behaviors to and tended to forget the behaviors more quickly.

## A THREE-STEP APPROACH

Many managers or supervisors understand the need to praise

as well as reprimand. Many, however, are unsure how to do it. Try this three step approach:

1. *Praise people on a one-to-one basis.* Jealously may develop if others witness your compliments and feel you are showing preferential treatment. After all, most people crave compliments.

2. *Be specific with your praise.* Tell the person exactly what you like; don't force them to guess. Don't say, "Good job." Say instead, "I like the way you presented the graphics in our portfolio. It was first rate." People are likely to repeat behaviors as long as they know what you approve of. Also, praise them for skills you want them to develop.

Single out an area you would like improved. But praise them first for activities they are doing correctly. They'll pay greater attention to that job and probably concentrate more on other aspects as well.

3. *Touch the person unobtrusively when you give them praise.* A light pat on the shoulder or a brief touch on the elbow will give your words more impact than a pile driver. Research by the University of Minnesota has shown that you can be much more persuasive if you touch people lightly as you talk. Their research indicated that people tend to remember messages reinforced in this manner longer than a verbal message alone.

## HOW TO REPRIMAND

While praise is important, it is sometimes necessary to also reprimand. Reprimand people only when you want them to make a quick change in behavior, but do it sparingly. Do it in a way that they'll accept and appreciate. Consider this approach:

1. *Invite the person into your office and close the door.* Never, never, never reprimand people in front of their peers. It will only serve to cause embarassment and resentment.

2. *Be specific with your reprimand.* This will help your message to be understood and taken as constructive criticism. Also be sincere and honest with your comments. Give the employee a chance to talk.

Rather than saying to your secretary, "You really irritated my client. Why did you do that? Thanks a lot," try a sincere and specific reprimand such as, "You really irritated my client. You were curt and abrasive. It was a long distance call and you left him on hold for five minutes. Please communicate with callers at least every thirty seconds and let them decide whether to continue holding."

3. *Lastly, praise their overall performance.* Touch them unobtrusively. Be firm with the reprimand but afterward be sure to praise them about their performance overall. As you talk about your faith in them, reinforce your words with a gentle touch. Make them feel that you care about them and want to help them improve. Don't praise them first, then "sock it to them" later. For example, "Jean, you've really been great here for the last six months, but if you ever hang up on my boss again, I'll fire you." A praise before a reprimand will cause suspicion even when you're praising others without the reprimand.

One of the toughest human relation lessons to learn is to criticize and reprimand people. But at the same time, if the employee or associate doesn't feel good about the way you deliver your criticism, they're unlikely to change.

A financial executive wrote me recently saying that he had used these techniques with his secretary. He had to ask her to take a 25 percent salary cut because of a business downturn. Even though she was often approached by job recruiters, she chose to stay with the executive. Why? Because of her employer's effectiveness in dealing with her.

Whether you're a marketer, manager, salesman or mother, these techniques may help you be more successful with people. Reward is an aspect of work people like most, and sincere praise can reap more benefits than money.

In the next chapter, we will discuss group presentations and ways of communicating effectively with your audience.

# PART 24

## FIVE STEPS TO GREAT PRESENTATIONS

Jim, a sales manager, was asked to give a ninety-minute speech to a regional sales meeting. His speech was to be an overview of why his producers were consistently among the top in the company. Weeks before, Jim painstakingly spent hours thinking, outlining, and organizing his comments. Not only was he petrified of speaking, but he had little confidence that his remarks would be of interest. When he gave his speech, just like a self-fulfilling prophecy, his audience tapped their pencils, lost attention, and daydreamed through his entire presentation. What happened? Even a man as sharp as Jim wasn't able to sufficiently communicate the techniques that made him one of the outstanding managers in the company.

Great mass communicators truly command not only organizations, but also the respect and admiration of people. Being an excellent speaker is and always has been a quick ride to the top — ask any politician. But, as you may already know, few people are naturally gifted speakers. In my own career, I spent nearly two years of sleepless nights worrying about my presentations the next day. If I knew then what I am about to share with you, I would have been far more effective and comfortable with any audience.

## THE FIVE-STEP PLAN

Try to incorporate one of these five steps every five minutes during your next group communication:

1. *Ask a rhetorical question of the group and then pause.* This communicates a number of important benefits. You will grab the group's attention by asking them to think about an answer. You will also let them know that you will be solving a problem. It is one of the best ways for a speaker to generate interest. For example, during one of my presentations, I asked the rhetorical question, "How many of you have had trouble 'getting through' to a prospect?" Not only did the attendees raise their hands, but they also voiced a humorous "yes" response in unison. The audience immediately sensed a benefit to be gained by listening to my presentation. An old adage in speaking suggests that if you don't grab the audience in the first five minutes, you may lose them until the last five minutes (when they sense you are closing).

2. *Use your own personal experiences to illustrate points.* Most groups don't want a "book report" by an amateur when an expert is readily available. If you convey the feeling that you have lived the concepts you are preaching, the audience will retain a much higher level of interest. In a presentation a few years ago, I discussed a concept called, "The Fear of Success." As an illustration, I talked about one of my past professional tennis matches in Rome, Italy, against the Italian national champion in the Italian Open. In the second set, the Italian fans, sensing that their hometown champion was losing, threw Italian lira down on the stadium clay court. The umpire postponed the match until the coins could be picked up. Jubil-

ant that I was finally getting paid, I sat down next to my doubles partner and bragged that the spectators were so enthralled with my playing that they threw money in appreciation. My partner told me that it was not appreciation the fans were showing; the lira they were throwing were practically worthless. The fans were, instead, communicating an old Italian omen: If I beat their hometown boy, Panatta, I wouldn't make it out of the parking lot. That's what I call a real "Fear of Success." By illustrating your concepts, with personal stories or experiences, you have given the audience part of yourself. You have shared your personality. Audiences will put as much value in this as they do in your content. Besides causing the group to increase their interest, you have helped them understand your ideas much more quickly.

3. *Get the audience to participate.* As I speak around the country, I notice that groups are tired of being lectured to or talked at — they want to be involved. They want to be part of the program. One of the reasons teleconferencing has not caught on, according to *Megatrend's* John Naisbitt is that it is not "high touch" enough. But, when a group does show up, they want more involvement than just watching a live version of a video presentation. They want to experience it.

## INVOLVE YOUR AUDIENCE

There are many ways you can help a group experience a presentation:

a) *The best way is to intermittently call audience members by name or even bring attendees up to the front of the room.* I have included this direct participation in my "How To Read Your Client's Mind" presentation. I bring at least four people to the front, one at a time, throughout the program to illustrate my concepts. Nothing will do more to increase your listener's attention than to watch "one of their own" participating in the program.

b) *An easier way would be to get the group to raise their hands in response to questions.*

c) *Better yet, shed the security of the podium and walk among the audience as you speak.* Phil Donahue, in his popular talk show, has made a career of walking through the audience, microphone in hand. Granted, Donahue is basically facilitating questions to the guest expert, but, more than that, he is able to involve his group so deeply that the studio audience waiting list is months long. Get a roving microphone and walk among the group. You don't need notes. Why not jot down one-word memory joggers and leave them on the front row seat. No one will sit in the front row anyway.

4. *Use humor to conclude every major point.* In memory retention studies at San Diego State University, researchers found that when ideas are associated with humor, they are remembered not only longer, but retained with much more detail than those ideas presented without humor. In fact, Johnny Carson once said that people will pay much more to be entertained than they will to be educated. While you are not likely an aspiring comedian, a touch of humor is bound to enhance any message that you give. Your attendees want to enjoy and feel good about your speech no matter what the topic. When you use humor, you break down suspicion, rid skepticism, as well as other psychological barriers that prevent your listeners from "buying" your ideas. I recently spoke at the annual convention of the International Association of Financial Planners. I presented a message full of very sophisticated and new client relations research. Nonetheless, I pumped humor in about every five minutes. Not only did the audience learn something, but numerous attendees told me that the reason they came to my program was because they heard it was enjoyable and fun.

I recommend that you use one-liners woven into personal stories. If they are illustrative of your point, you'll be evaluated as not only a bright speaker, but also charismatic. Charismatic speakers make an audience feel good as well as giving valuable content. A great place to get humorous one-liners is to attend your local comedy night clubs. I get a lot of good ideas for humor from these young comedians that I then adapt for my own use. Another great place to get humor is from Bob Orben's series of books on humor for speakers. He has put together some of the funniest topical one-liners I have ever seen.

5. *Never present more than four or five major ideas at any one sitting.* Amateur and inexperienced speakers simply try to cram too much into a very short amount of time. They end up treating their subject superficially. The only way they could say less is to speak longer. Avoid this mistake. The mind can absorb only what the seat can endure. The seat will endure a lot more if you properly present only four to five major ideas at one time. Of course, the length of time you speak depends on the entertainment value. I'm often asked how long one should speak before a break. A good rule of thumb (if you're using my Five Steps to Great Presentations), is to speak no more than ninety minutes. Without using my steps, twenty to thirty minutes is about the maximum.

Bertram Shuster, a well-to-do asset manager in Chicago, recently heard me at a financial planning conference. He picked up my newsletter and read "Five Steps to Great Presentations." That evening, he changed the speech that he was preparing for the same conference. He incorporated the five steps. He approached me after his speech and said that in ten years of delivering presentations, for the first time, he had a dozen or so attendees tell him that they not only found his content interesting but truly enjoyed listening to him. They all said they could have listened for another couple of hours!

If you present well in front of groups, you command more influence and power. More importantly, your great ideas deserve great delivery. These five techniques for presenting effectively will help you affect more people positively in one hour than you could see face-to-face in weeks.

Just as I have outlined five steps to effective group presentations, in the following chapter I will detail five characteristics that mark the peak performers in sales.

# PART 25

# THE FIVE CHARACTERISTICS OF PEAK PERFORMERS

Are you a peak sales performer? As I have traveled around the globe, I've noticed that every salesperson I contact tells me that they are the best in the world. Nobody else can sell or close like them. But yet, when I press them on exactly what it is that makes up a peak sales producer, they usually say a strong mental attitude, goals, and aspirations. It's shocking to see what little knowledge most salespeople have of actually what it takes to be a top producer in the sales field.

The Xerox Coporation conducted a nationwide study to learn what top performers were doing. This study outlined the behavioral differences among salespeople in over twenty-four different industries. They studied over 500 sales calls, looking at top producing sales performers as well as mediocre and extremely marginal producers. They found five different behavior patterns that seemed to characterize the most successful salespeople in the world. Would you like to find out what those five characteristics are? You'll be surprised at how simple, yet profound they are.

## THE FIVE BASIC CHARACTERISTICS

### A BALANCED DIALOGUE

These peak sales producers first *establish a balanced dialogue* very quickly with their prospect and interact like friends. They seem to have an uncanny way of getting their prospect involved and helping their prospect discover why their product or service would be of value in solving their problems. They also realize that proving how the product will be valuable is much better than just telling the prospect about it. In other parts of this book, I have tried to make it very obvious that your prospect will never buy because of what you present. He, instead buys from what he convinces himself of. This means that even if you are selling a watch, telling that prospect a watch will help cure his problem of not knowing what time it is will not be enough. Your prospect needs to discover for himself that this watch will indeed keep him from running late. He will not listen to you, he will only listen to himself.

A short time ago I bought a BMW 535 sportscar. I'd been looking at cars for three months until I came upon one I really liked. This 535 was so powerful, as the salesman said, that it could blow the doors off a 911 Porsche. Well, I didn't believe this, nor did it even evoke a smile from me when I heard it. But the salesman put me into the car. He sat in the back seat as my wife sat in the front seat. In Manhattan Beach, California, I took this five-speed BMW through it's paces. As soon as I shifted out of first into second gear, my wife screamed at me and said she was getting whiplash. I suddenly realized that the salesman was right when he talked about the power of this car. It occurred to me on the spot how much this car felt like a racer. I bought it one week later.

## ASKING QUESTIONS SKILLFULLY

The second characteristic of peak performing salespeople is their *ability to ask questions skillfully to gather information and uncover their prospects' and customers' needs.* These top sales producers are so good at probing that they always uncover their prospects' needs first, before they mention anything about the product. I'm sure you have found as I have that if you talk about the product benefits or the price too soon, the prospect often disqualifies you by saying it's not for him. But these top producers will acknowledge and support the prospects' comments twice as fast as mediocre performers. They have an uncanny way of using what psychologists call *counseling techniques,* to ferret out the prospect's true needs and wants. These *top performers ask 25 percent more open-ended questions than the low performers.* I'm sure you have been contacted before by stock brokers or insurance agents who possess an image of being a hard closer. The reason they seem pushy is because they have not yet developed enough rapport with you to actually recommend what you should buy. They have not listened to your needs before they prescribe a solution. Well, these top salespeople are so good at probing that they make you think they know your problem inside and out before they ever recommend a solution.

I recently called a life insurance manager for a very large company in the United States. I wanted to speak at his next conference. Springboarding from a very strong referral, I probed for just a few minutes. He seemed to do almost all the talking and basically told me three times in the first four minutes that they already had a sales psychologist on board that was serving their needs quite well. Undaunted, I simply listened to the manager's comments throughout the balance of the interview. I then said that I wanted to be involved in speaking at their next conference if he thought I would contribute. Just before I hung up, this manager said, "The reason I didn't hang up on you in the first few minutes is because you are such a good listener. I couldn't help but think, Kerry, that if somebody listens that well to our needs, they can certainly help us solve our problems."

## MATCHING PRODUCT TO NEED

Third, peak sales performers have *great skill at matching their product features to the prospects' needs.* They have learned to uncover real needs and show how the product or service can satisfy them. These peak performers are so good at uncovering needs that they often find more than one. In fact, research has now shown that when two or more needs were discovered, a sale occurred. Many of us in the sales business have a tendency to present benefits that don't relate to immediate needs. Unfortunately, if you talk about product benefits and features that do not match up to the needs of your prospect, you are inviting objections.

A short time ago, I talked to a prospect of mine over the telephone who told me he wanted a training package on ideas that would help him close more effectively. I discussed an audio tape program entitled, "How To Read Your Client's Mind," for about two or three minutes. I went on to say that it would help him listen more effectively and aid him in being more persuasive. I said this in addition to the information I gave him on how it will help him close. He promptly gave me an objection and said, "Gee, I'm not sure I need more information on listening, I think I'm a pretty good listener already." He was in effect saying to me that I actually presented benefits that did not correspond to his needs. I probed him effectively and understood what he wanted, but, I didn't match up my product benefits to his needs as closely as he wanted.

## TURNING A NEGATIVE ATTITUDE AROUND

These peak sales performers have a fourth characteristic. *They have a highly developed talent at turning a prospect's negative attitude around.* These top sales producers have found an interesting technique of being able to counter objections and a prospect's rejection properly and directly. Do you receive objections when you sell? This is a fairly obvious question. It's like asking if fish can breathe under water. But during psychological studies, it was shown that successful sales calls contain 50 percent more objections than those appointments that result in no sale. What this indicates is that the people who buy will produce more objections than people who will not buy. It seems clear then that it's not the prospect who is giving up by saying, "I don't want it," it's more likely you quit too early in the sales process. You may be quitting before the prospect does.

There are actually three ways to answer objections: before they're asked, when they are asked and after they're asked. You obviously know that some prospects will give you objections nearly every time you present a product. Knowing when those objections may come up will undoubtedly give you a key advantage in addressing them before they arise. "Mr. Prospect, some people have even said that this typewriter ribbon does not last as long as other ribbons on the market, but we have found that the high quality allows it to be reused, many times." If you answer the objection before it is asked, you will cut out a source of frustration.

The obvious time to answer an objection is when it's asked. The only time you would ignore an objection is if the prospect is being frivolous or flamboyant. I once received an objection from a company vice president who said, "We are firing all of our salespeople next week. We are then replacing them with new people. So I will not need your services." This was a foolish and flamboyant objection because he basically said that his current salespeople were so poorly trained and so poorly motivated, he had to get new people. All his woes would be cured with his new hires. This is not reality. The same thing that happened to his past salespeople will also happen to his new ones.

A good time to answer an objection is after it is asked. Undoubtedly, you have received objections in which a prospect said something like, "Well, how much does this cost anyway?" or, "This is way too expensive; I can't afford it." The objection may come at a point when you have not been able to fully give the prospect a sense of value for what he's buying. You might simply say, "I'll get to how I can justify the cost in a few minutes.

I once heard a computer salesperson get an objection from a prospect in the middle of the presentation. The prospect said, "I haven't got an air conditioning unit that can support a computer this big in my office." The salesperson promptly said, "I understand your concern and in just a couple of seconds, I will show you why it won't really be a problem." So rather than let that prospect distract him, he was able to thereby circumvent the objection and address it at a later time when it would better fit into the presentation and make more sense.

## POST CLOSING

The fifth and last characteristic of peak sales performers is one of *knowing how to post close*. Top producers have learned to summarize benefits and propose a concise and succinct plan of action when they close. There is a difference between the peak performers and the marginal performers in this one characteristic. The poor performers tend to sell their product, thereby cutting off all contact after the sale with their prospect. This leaves the prospect with the sense that he is high and dry with no recourse if something goes wrong. The top performer actually lays a plan of action, helping the prospect understand exactly what will happen in implementing his product. He also communicates that the relationship will continue after the product is purchased. They in effect are saying, "Mr. Prospect, by buying this product, our relationship is just starting, not ending. The is where the real effort comes in in servicing you, helping you get what you want and solving your problems."

The Xerox study actually showed that when this kind of proposed type of close was used, 75 percent of the prospects ending up buying. This tells you that your prospect not only wants your product, but he wants to know that you come with the purchase. He wants to continue the relationship. It is important to know and understand that when your prospect buys, he is saying, "I'm buying your trust and the rapport we've had together. I'm buying the product benefits second." Now this may change in certain situations. If you are buying a product over the telephone or through direct mail, the need for a strong relationship may not be as high. But when a prospect says to you, "I want to buy your product," he is basically saying, "I trust you, I think a lot of you, I want to spend time with you afterward. Please support and keep that relationship strong after I buy this product."

Here are some other key items from the Xerox research:
1) The age, sex, and experience level of the salesperson did not significantly affect whether the prospect will buy. Whether that salesperson was eighteen or eighty, male or female, the prospect was as likely to buy because of these five characteristics than whether that person was thirty, male with ten years experience.
2) The study showed that the ability of the salesperson to recognize cues like buying signals and using skillful techniques in controlling the call were much more beneficial than having

the best product. The communication skills of these top sales people, more than made up for not having the best product on the market.

3) By looking at poor producing salespeople, it was shown that marginal performers tend to overstructure the sales call. The biggest mistake they make is to think of a sales call as one in which their prospect only cared about their product. The top performers seem to move smoothly into establishing a dialogue and rapport, thereby maintaining a strong relationship and controlling the call.

This is also very true of my marketing director, Joy. When she first joined my office, I found that she was talking to my prospects about what Kerry Johnson could offer as a speaker at their next conference. When I listened to one of her phone calls, I found out that she was totally ignoring the relationship and talking only about the product. But after learning this, I told her to spend at least a few moments talking about the location of the program, the academy awards, football, baseball, or even tennis, for at least a few moments before she jumped into the product itself. The relationship is always more important than the product. If that were not true then cars could be sold through direct mail. It was also found that average salespeople tend to be inefficient in dealing with information about a prospect's needs. They often are given good questions to ask by their managers but apparently don't listen well enough or take advantage of the information received. They concentrate too hard on asking the right questions instead of listening to the responses.

## ESTABLISHING A DIALOGUE

And lastly, the top performing sales people were able to *establish a dialogue very easily and control it subtly*. They were very alert to closing opportunities, known as buying signals, throughout the interview. Often you'll find your prospects show buying signals, such as leaning forward in their chairs, putting a hand on their knee and forearm on their thigh, as well as pupils dilating. This was discussed in another chapter in this book. On the telephone, buying signals are cues such as the voice modulating up saying words like, "Really, sounds good to me," or, "Great." These top performing salespeople are very attuned to these nuances. They know when they've said enough, it's time to close.

I hope these research findings have given you a better concept of how peak performers sell and how they handle relationships. It's not enough to just present a product, you have to be a psychologist of sorts in knowing how to read the prospect very quickly, even in the first few moments of interaction. The successful sales call lasts thirty-three minutes on the average. The successful salesperson asks an average of 13.6 questions, describes an average of 6.4 product benefits, and lists over 7.7 product features. So you can see that there's a lot more listening and questioning done than actually presenting the product. The prospect, on the other hand, usually gives the salesperson about 2.2 different needs, raises 1.4 objections and makes 2.8 statements of acceptance while asking 7.7 questions of his own. The point here is that, yes, you will get objections. But if you uncover their needs and allow prospects to give you acceptance statements, they will buy and you will sell. Read your prospects both verbally and non-verbally. Think about these characteristics and then analyze your own sales efforts. Take an inventory of your strengths and weaknesses.

When I was on the pro tennis tour, I never played a match without asking someone to list the number of unforced errors I hit, my first serve percentage, and the number of winning backhands and forehands I hit. After the tennis match, this allowed me to analyze my performance and work on the parts of my game that were the weakest.

If you can analyze your sales game and discover which are strongest and the weakest, selling for you will be as natural as Reggie Jackson hitting a home run in October. You'll be astonished when someone says, "No." Use these techniques and you will produce more sales than you have in a long time.

The final chapter contains letters and response to my various magazine articles. Perhaps you'll find an answer or two to your questions here.

# PART 26

## ADVICE TO THE SALESLORN

During the past few years, I have received numerous letters to my many magazine articles. Most are sincere questions relating to concerns readers have about their sales or management effectiveness. I have always been surprised to see the same questions asked over and over again. I'm sure that you'll read about problems and concerns you also have had or are currently having. This "Ann Landers" style advice will hopefully entertain you, but, also let you know that we all suffer the same problems and business frustrations.

*Dear Kerry:*

*I seem to have trouble obtaining referrals. Each time it is appropriate to ask, the words just get stuck on my tongue. And when I do ask, I am uncomfortable if there is silence while the person thinks of a name. What can I do?*

*Tongue-Tied In Tustin*

Dear Tongue Tied In Tustin:

Obtaining referrals effectively is the life blood of many sales-oriented businesses. Without referrals, you may force yourself to exist on less productive cold calls. Unfortunately, many salespeople experience difficulty asking for leads. This insecurity stems from a fear that if the client says no to the referral request, he's rejecting you. You may feel that if you give him the opportunity to say no to your request, he may terminate the relationship. Your irrational thought might be, "If the client really wanted to give me a referral, he would volunteer it." In reality, your client doesn't know you want referrals unless you to ask for them. He's probably willing to give you as many referrals as you want.

The best technique in asking for referrals is to be very specific with your request. Rather than ask, "Mr. Client, would you give me a few referrals?" say instead, "Would you please give me three people whom you know well and who could benefit from the kind of service I have given you?" By asking for three names, you have presented him with a clear objective to achieve. Also, by asking for those who could gain from your service, you can, in effect prospect by saying, "John thought I might be able to help you improve employee benefits program." And don't overlook referral requests from prospects who reject you. Like clients, you'll find them willing to refer you to someone who might have a greater need for your services. *The definition of a great salesman is one who has the ability to make cold calls but never needs to.*

272

*Dear Kerry:*

*Most of the time my first interviews go well. I promise to consider any problems that are uncovered and develop appropriate solutions. However, when I try to reach the party to obtain a second appointment, I often have trouble getting through to the prospect or having my calls returned. Granted, these people own their own businesses and are generally quite busy, but I never know if they are really busy or are avoiding me. How can I tell?*

*Ostracized in Orange County*

Dear Ostracized:

The real reason you have a tough time following up is simply the common prospect opinion, "There's no hurry." The sales cycle consists of not just one close but frequent closes throughout the transaction. You already close on a prospecting phone call to book an appointment. You also should close on booking a second appointment. Recently, a prospect I called said he'd like me to speak to his company in June. He didn't know the specific date. Rather than requesting he call back later in the year, I said, "Is the second or third week in June better for you? Which day is more likely — Thursday or Friday?" If he had balked at my close, I would have said, "I can follow up more easily when I have a target date to shoot for whether or not it may change." Follow-up appointments should be conducted in the same way.

Rules for follow-up are: 1) Ask for a home phone number. You may never use it, but it's another way of qualifying your prospect. "Mr. Prospect, just in case I can't reach you at the office next week, what is your home phone number?" This may be more effective for personal products like life insurance than in a corporate situation. 2) Book the second appointment during the first meeting. "Shall we meet next Monday at 3, or is 4 better?" 3) When you must telephone to schedule a follow-up appointment, leave a specific message. Your prospect may not put a high priority on returning a call to a salesperson, John Smith. He is more likely to return a call if the message reads, "John Smith would like to see you Friday at 3 p.m. for a follow-up appointment." Your prospect may appreciate having the follow-up appointment scheduled for him.

*Dear Kerry:*

*In selling face-to-face, there is often a need to gently push the prospect into purchasing. Even using a fact finder and selling on a needs basis creates this situation: I am so concerned with not being pushy that I don't close nearly as well as I'd like to. I hate being pushed, so I don't like to push others. Can you help me?*

*Reluctant In Reno*

Dear Reluctant:

The latest research indicates that over 30 percent of potential sales are lost because of not closing. This is simply an inability to ask that prospect to buy. Another 40 percent of sales are lost because the salesperson didn't close at the right time. Craig Beachnaw in Lansing, Michigan, nearly lost a $20,000 commission sale. After he closed the deal, Craig asked the prospect what he said that was influential in closing the sale. The prospect said, "Actually, I was ready to buy one hour before you stopped talking. To be honest, you were talking me out of it."

Close any way you like, but close. The two best techniques are assumptive and alternate of choice. The assumptive technique merely states that the prospect will stop you from writing up the order if he doesn't want to buy. The alternate of choice close works like this: "Mr Prospect, is $500,000 or $600,00 of whole life more appealing to you right now?" It is a rare case that a prospect will actually say, "Yes, I want to buy." But they often appreciate help in fighting their allergy to yes.

If you close at the wrong time your prospect may feel a

psychological emotion known as "interview stress." The best closers in the country will close until they see one of three defensive signals. When your prospect is feeling pushed, pressed, and closed, he will: 1) blink his eyes very rapidly; 2) break eye contact for more than just a few seconds; 3) rub his forehead from side to side. If you see any of these gestures, you can expect rejection from him. If he shows these nuances, stop talking and elicit emotion. "Don, how do you feel about this so far? What are you really thinking? Is there something here that is bothering you?" If you sell, don't be afraid to close. If you watch your prospect's buying readiness, you'll never lose a sale because you've pushed the prospect too hard.

*Dear Kerry:*

*I often have problems getting to the decision maker in a business sale. The people I work with in these situations claim to be the decision makers until the closing moment comes. What should I do?*

*Powerless in Provo*

Dear Powerless:

Getting through to the decision maker is job number one. We frequently are relegated down to a functionary who simply decides whether we can have access to the decision maker. More often than not, this person screens us. In your case, though, the decision maker seems to be giving you an objection that says, "I'm not the guy." This is a frequent ploy used in negotiations. A player might say, "I'm sorry, I have to check with my committee and I'll get back to you." Management expert Peter Drucker once said a committee is an anarchy held together by a parking lot. Recently I was approached by a broker attempting to sell disability insurance. After he explained his product over the telephone, I said, "I really don't make these kinds of decisions." I could have said yes, but I didn't have the time or the motivation to discuss his product. I referred him to my wife. I fully realized my wife would check back with me. From now on, after qualifying a prospect, say, "Who will make this decision with you?" If they say, "Tom," you may be talking to the wrong guy. If he states, "Just me," that objection won't come up. Another technique is one from the stock brokerage business. These smile and dialers often ask, "If I found a great idea, would you be able to invest $20,000 in it today?" If the answer is no, you've saved yourself time. In any business, we could say, "If you found this beneficial, could you make a decision on it today?"

Most importantly, get your prospect to acknowledge, ahead of time, who is the decision maker. If it's not the person you're talking with, get permission (an official referral) to talk to the right prospect. Then qualify their power to make a decision ahead of time, not at the time you try to close.

*Dear Dr. Johnson:*

*I'm new to the business and may be creating my own dilemmas: However, all too frequently, I find myself in less-than-advantageous selling situations - standing at counters, reviewing proposals with frequent interruptions by employees and/or phones or having much less time given than required. Results are a too quick overview of the proposal and too little time to arrive at the point of decision. Then when we have rescheduled at a later date and meet again, the whole need and concept must be totally reestablished. Tell me, is this just a lack of control on my part? If so, how can I establish greater control? What do I say and/or do?*

*For What It's Worth*

Dear For What It's Worth:

Your dilemma seems to be one of a rushed prospect who has not yet bought into the need. He has failed to perceive the necessity of your interviews as well as underestimating the time needed. From now on try to let your prospect know up front what you will be doing. During the initial appointment, inform him of the steps you will go through to effectively satisfy his needs.

You're not giving your prospect a true image of yourself as a busy person who should be respected as such. Present yourself as a professional who knows what you are doing and has many other clients. Let your prospect know, at the onset, how you will help him. Get them to agree to take action on the goals you both set. If your prospect knows you are thorough in your efforts to help him, he won't waste your valuable time.

## A FINAL THOUGHT

Throughout this book, you have been given ideas on selling and leading people that stem from the newest research in psychology. But the fact still remains: products don't sell themselves, people do. Is it not true that 90 percent of your training time is spent learning about products and their technical applications. 10 percent of training time is spent learning about how to deal with people. But yet 90 percent of your day is spent dealing with people and only 10 percent in actively applying the product information. If this were not so, automobiles, houses, and loans could be sold by mail order bypassing the salesperson. Sell solutions, not products. Solve problems instead of manipulate. When people feel that you are an expert who cares about them, they'll beat a path to your door. Your prospect doesn't trust the product, he trusts you and will buy whatever you recommend.

## PERSONAL APPEARANCES

Dr. Kerry Johnson has become one of America's most sought after speakers. He presents programs over 15 times each month to some of the world's largest corporations and most prestigious associations. His presentations are packed with useful and transferable ideas, seasoned with humor and audience participation.

For more information about scheduling Kerry Johnson to address your group, call or write:

Kerry L. Johnson, Ph.D.
International Productivity Systems, Inc.
P.O. Box 3665
Tustin, California 92681-3665
(714) 730-3560